Lee Harwood was born in 1939  Surrey. Since 1963 he has edited a magazines' and given poetry readir the United States, Canada, Fran During the past 20 years he has pub... several volumes of translation, including Tristan ... *Selected Poems*, and had his work included in numerous anthologies. He lives in Brighton, Sussex.

'Lee Harwood is concerned with precision, stories begun, expeditions set up, landscapes are glimpsed; but to a purpose – to explore a personal statement of a state of mind, to revitalize language and stock phrases by a context that fires on broken lines, retracted and undercut statements, movements toward a perfection, precision and elegance, whose elusiveness sparks the wider implications of the poem, i.e. those outside the question of language. These books are landmarks in the development of English poetry.'
Paul Selby *Poetry Information*

LEE HARWOOD

Crossing the Frozen River

Selected Poems

PALADIN
GRAFTON BOOKS
A Division of the Collins Publishing Group

LONDON GLASGOW
TORONTO SYDNEY AUCKLAND

Paladin
Grafton Books
A Division of the Collins Publishing Group
8 Grafton Street, London W1X 3LA

A Paladin Paperback Original 1988

The poems in this collection originally appeared in: Adam, Alembic, Ambit, Angel Hair, Ant's Forefoot, Bezoar, Big Venus, Blatant Acts of Poetry, Blocks, Bones, The Boston Phoenix, The Brighton & Hove Gazette, Broadsheet, Collection, Converse, Cosmos, Eleventh Finger, The English Intelligencer, Fire Exit, Frice/Nice/Vice, Hand, Haravec, Honey magazine, In Folio, Inherited, Issue, Lettera, Local Colour, London Magazine, Luna Tack, Mandate, Michigan Quarterly, Molly Bloom, Montemora, New Measure, Ninth Decade, Oasis, Ochre, Oink, One, Palantir, Paris Review, Partisan Review, Perfect Bound, Poetry Review (London), Reality Studios, Rock Drill, Sesheta, Six Pack, Slow Dancer, Smoke, Soma, South East Arts Review, Staple Diet, Stonechat, Stone Soup, Telegram, Transatlantic Review, Tribune, TriQuarterly, Twelve to Twelve: Camden Festival 1970, Tzarad, Underground, United Artists, Windows, Wivenhoe Park Review, Work, The World, Writers Forum 100.

The poems were first published in book form in: *The Man with Blue Eyes* (Angel Hair Books, New York, 1966), *The White Room* (Fulcrum Press, London, 1968), *The beautiful atlas* (Kavanagh, Brighton, 1969), *Landscapes* (Fulcrum Press, 1969), *The Sinking Colony* (Fulcrum Press, 1970), *Captain Harwood's Log of Stern Statements and Stout Sayings* (Writers Forum, London, 1973), *HMS Little Fox* (Oasis Books, London, 1975), *Old Bosham Bird Watch & other stories* (Pig Press, Durham, 1977), *Boston to Brighton* (Oasis Books, 1977), *Wish You Were Here* (published together with a sequence by Antony Lopez) (Transgravity Press, Deal, 1979), *All the Wrong Notes* (Pig Press, 1981), *Faded Ribbons . . .* (Other Branch Readings, Leamington Spa, 1982) *Monster Masks* (Pig Press, 1985), and *Dream Quilt: 30 assorted stories* (Slow Dancer Press, Nottingham, 1985), *Rope Boy to the Rescue* (North and South, 1988).

'Text for two posters' was written in collaboration with the artist Ian Brown. The posters were commissioned and published by South East Arts in 1980.

My thanks to all these editors and publishers.   L.H.

ISBN 0-586-08704-4

Printed and bound in Great Britain by
Collins, Glasgow

Set in Meridian

My thanks and much more to John Ashbery, Paul Evans, Harry Guest and Marian O'Dwyer. Without their friendship over the years this collection would not have been possible.

Lee Harwood

'It is, I find, in zoology as it is in botany: all nature is so full, that that district produces the greatest variety which is the most examined'
Gilbert White, letter XX to Pennant, in
The Natural History of Selborne

'I do not know which of us has written this page'
Jorge Luis Borges *Borges and I*

Contents

Foreword

Lee Harwood's poetry lies open to the reader, like a meadow. It moves slowly towards an unknown goal, like a river. It is carelessly wise, that is, wise without knowing or caring what wisdom is. In these things it seems more like recent American poetry than English poetry. The English language is constantly trying to stave off an invasion by the American language; it lives in a state of alert which is reflected to some degree in English poetry. The American language does not know it is invading the English language and would not understand about this, since it considers all words desirable and is always borrowing or inventing new, not always necessary ones. Lee Harwood's English is like American English in that it lacks a strong sense of possession. At the same time it has a pearly, soft-focus quality one rarely sees in American poetry, and which I associate with poets like Wordsworth and Arnold. The 'great' poetry I like best has this self-effacing, translucent quality. Self-effacing not from modesty but because it is going somewhere and has no time to consider itself.

John Ashbery

The Man with Blue Eyes

As your eyes are blue . . .

As your eyes are blue   *olive green.*
you move me – and the thought of you –
I imitate you.
and cities apart. yet a roof grey with slates
or lead. the difference is little   *stolen land*
and even you could say as much
through a foxtail of pain   even you

when the river beneath your window
was as much as I dream of. loose change and
your shirt on the top of a chest-of-drawers
a mirror facing the ceiling and the light in a cupboard
left to burn all day   a dull yellow
probing the shadowy room   'what was it?'

'cancel the tickets' – a sleep talk
whose horrors razor a truth that can
walk with equal calm through palace rooms
chandeliers tinkling in the silence as winds batter the gardens
outside   formal lakes shuddering at the sight
of two lone walkers
                                of course this exaggerates
small groups of tourists appear and disappear
in an irregular rhythm of flowerbeds

you know even in the stillness of my kiss
that doors are opening in another apartment
on the other side of town   a shepherd grazing
his sheep through a village we know

high in the mountains the ski slopes thick with summer flowers
and the water-meadows below with narcissi
the back of your hand and –

Ambles Road

a newly designed red bus drives quietly down Gower Street
a brilliant red   'how could I tell you . . .'
with such confusion
                              meetings disintegrating
and a general lack of purpose only too obvious
in the affairs of state
                              'yes, it was on a hot july day
with taxis gunning their motors on the throughway
a listless silence in the backrooms of paris bookshops
why bother   one thing equal to another

dinner parties whose grandeur stops all conversation

but
        the afternoon sunlight which shone in
your eyes as you lay beside me watching for . . . –
we can neither remember – still shines as you
wait nervously by the window for the ordered taxi
to arrive   if only I could touch your naked shoulder
now   'but then . . .'

and the radio still playing the same
records I heard earlier today
                              – and still you move me
and the distance is nothing
'even you –

Before Schulz the Kiteman

Paris clambering through the chimney pots of your dreams
harpsichord slicing eggs
      into flowers
flowers into tumbrils
tumbrils into towers
towers bursting from lakes
        in remote mountain districts
a peasant walked dazed into the village
        a dog couldn't avoid his boots
     a hay stack collapsed
     crying
        when you passed

'oh it really twists within me' he said
a tear enveloped the village
I couldn't discipline my troops enough
so the campaign lagged through a winter schedule
rain obliterated a trail
     in a water sun
     a man emerged with rabbits in his shirt
and passed through the city walls
'let me tell you how this curse came upon us'
a dam was breached
and ever since people couldn't stop
you know the winter also collapsed in tears

walking along the avenues

my stomach arches you
and a love army marched across
occupying us hopelessly

this was only the beginning

For John in the mountains

In a mountain sun
pursued by my own phantoms
monsters lurking in the forest
                              in my head
an innocent forest out there
mountain flowers and meadows
the swirl of grass and pines hissing

at each open bush a terror
behind me   a dark snow
darker than your eyes'
dark snow
in which some flowers
can grow into me
a night when your river
could have left its bed
a desert awakening
a maniac pyramid
settle into a newness

your kiss holds such towns

No – all the temple bells . . .

No – all the temple bells
can only kneel
groans and chantings

a purity neither lost nor found
only a further dumbness with words

I can kneel here
        with no special ritual
but my own
a carpet design
        or a twisted heap of metal
my obsession god this minute

cymbals dulled drums
        my clothing so ornate that
        I have to move with ceremony
  gold and silver
        silks at my throat
a minute explosion puffing
from a small top window

whoever you are
let me shelter you

        and with this
        drumming rhythms grew
    until the entire planet was woven
                into

an elaborate stringball
rolling across a green desert
whose orange and humid night
I now eat and offer you

'let us reconsider . . . I mean these
mountain problems'
a car starting in a quiet side street

Lausanne 26 July 65

a cat twining itself round a mountain-top
the mountain crying
tears set in the long black fur
a lake so cold
that palms keep their respectful distance
on hotel balconies overlooking this scene

this couldn't be
yet the cat's eyes – I know – have shone
in so many towns
shadowing me and so many others

if lions tigers forests could spring
from such an earth

and the train's restaurant-car with
knowing smiles exchanged over the wine
and signals so often repeated
that they've lost their meaning
and the response becomes a mere formality

dark woods with orange creatures   *green leaves*
flitting through like forest rangers'   *with orange*
lanterns in the unending storm

but only repeating themselves
and other nights
and so lost again in the fur of nights
half-suffocated
but the plan always working out

and a head bursting from the lake
gasping
and catching breath
the submarine escape-hatch stuck
but a way round this difficulty was found
always given that last chance
when the pressure gets too much

so the idiot's grin and the calm return
of the sailors to their ship
and the mountain curling round the same
or another cat
in its well-meant and sadly clumsy fashion

The white and blue liner left harbour and began to cross the ocean again

the lone hunger of wolves on ice blue days
a sleigh with tugging yapping dogs passed through the forest
and I was still nowhere near you
autumn was the same in seaside towns
as it was in the dark mill-town valleys of the north
the rain beating down on the sodden hill-side
to tell you of the warmth indoors seems
too irrelevant –
                a kiss gone forever
is too easy to understand that I have to stay
silent
the leap back into cafes and juke-boxes   *Spanish*
again is too simple a reaction that I   *city*
follow it and am surprised that it works   *Whitley*
                                               Bay

'the deserted houses and empty windows
what can I say'

just fold it up and pack away
a tangle of circumstances

Summer

these hot afternoons 'it's quite absurd' she whispered
sunlight stirring her cotton dress inside the darkness when
an afternoon room crashed not breaking a bone or flower.
a list of cities crumbled under riots and distant gun-fire
yet the stone buildings sparkle. It is not only
the artificial lakes in the parks . . . perhaps . . .
but various illusions of belonging fall with equal noise and
    regularity
how could they know, the office girls as well
'fancy falling for him . . .' and inherit a sickness
such legs fat and voluptuous . . . smiling to himself
the length of train journeys

the whole landscape of suburban railway tracks,
passive canals and coloured oil-refineries.
it could be worse –

at intervals messages got through
the senate was deserted all that summer
black unmarked airplanes would suddenly appear
and then leave the sky surprised at its quiet
'couldn't you bear my tongue in your mouth?'

skin so smooth in the golden half-light
I work through nervousness to a poor but
convincing appearance of bravery and independence

mexico crossed by railways. aztec ruins
finally demolished and used for spanning one more ravine
in a chain of mountain tunnels and viaducts

and not one tear to span her grief
to lick him in the final mad-house hysteria
of armour falling off, rivets flying in all directions like fire-
   crackers
and the limp joy of the great break-down
which answers so many questions.
a series of lovers – but could you? –
all leading through the same door after the first hours
of confused ecstasies.
the dream woman who eats her lover.
would suffocation be an exaggeration of what really happens?
the man who forgets, leaving the shop
without his parcels, but meaning no harm.
'it's all a question of possession,
jealousy and . . .' the ability to torment,
the subtle bullying of night long talkings.
what artificial fruits can compare with this
and the wrecked potting-sheds that lie open
throughout the land? gorging their misery
and that of others . . . geranium flowers hacked off the plants
by gentlemen's canes and now limp on the gravel
   paths wandering through empty lawns and shrubberies
afternoon bickerings on a quiet park bench while
families take tea at a convenient cafe, so nicely situated.

engines and greased axles clattering through the shunting-
   yards.
fluttering parasols running for cover
under the nearby elms as the first heavy sweet raindrops
lick the girls forehead. the slightly hysterical
conversations crowded beneath the leaking branches
waiting for the july thunder to pass. The damp heat
and discomfort of clothes. a tongue passing the length
of her clitoris . . . and back again . . .
erections in the musty pavilion which should lead to a lake
but doesn't. the resin scent and dry throat in the pine wood
across the meadows.
                    'surely you remember?'
but so long ago.

strawberries lining her lake in the dark woods
an old picture slowly fading on the wall
as if a flower too could change her face
as a dusk cloaks our loneliness

That evening Pierre insisted that I had two roast pigeons at dinner

The loon house woke up
it was as if in the late afternoon and the exercise was repeated
some days when the streets were overgrown
the odd mail coach got through and a
bear was sighted on the outskirts of the marsh town
your sentimentality is better now than
    the earlier cynicism complaining at the
quality of omelettes

that solitary flag on the skyline and the
grey public buildings that surround the park
how you hated me but now we could embrace
it was and you saw it sunday papers
spread over your bed and my shy clumsy introduction
fleeing to another's arms usage can mean safety
I can tell this from photos
hasn't this battle field been too often re-visited

'hasn't this fool game gone on too long?'
we locked the hut up for the last time
and walked back down through the pine forest
the melting snow-line a thing of the past

Interrogation

1

a crackling in the next room
the officer quickly rose
I could hear him talking quietly

we folded the house
        and moved to another site

2

the plain was deserted
a few stunted fir trees
the first snow falling
mottling the landscape

that day it was my duty
to polish the sledge runners

I sang quietly as I worked
my breath in small clouds
the barn empty
it was then that

3

a list slowly mounting
crossed out
remounting

a cherokee fusillade
in his eyes
a warm hand
suddenly found in the bed

4

'you will either say A or B'

     I could see he was getting angry

'you will either say YES or NO,
you do or you don't –
you understand me don't you?'

     his distress was painful to watch

     I left the room
     and danced on my own
     to rock'n'roll records
     slowly in a larger room

     a temporary block was achieved

'you see we have to know . . .
'it is useless your continuing like this . . .
'we can help you . . . you need our help . . .'

     he was practising in the next room
     he worked so hard

     did he ever rest?

5

or was it that fencing job
          over by Snake Creek
must get me some new gloves
that wire can rip a glove apart in a week or less

6

the snow began to settle
and I returned to the main room
the table was set
we began again

but first a quiet
the wind outside
the transmitter humming
the officer finishing his cigarette
I sat in the usual place
the light was set
the papers sorted
we began again

it was still very quiet outside.

Landscape with 3 people

1

When the three horsemen rode in
you left me
there was no great pain at your leaving
if I am quite honest
you disappeared back into the house
and I mounted up and rode out with the men

It is strange that now many years later
aboard this whaler I should remember
your pink dress and the crash of the screen door

2

The roses tumbled down through the blue sky
and it was time for us to go out
Our horses were saddled and the peon waited patiently
The morning was still cool and quiet – a low
mist was still staring at our horses' hooves.
So we rode round the estate till 10 o'clock
– all was well.

Later at my desk – the accounts settled – I would
take a thin book of poems and read
till he brought me my dry martini
heavy ice cubes clattering in the tumbler
and vodka like sky-trailers gradually
accepting the vermouth and sky.
but this was a different ranch

and my dreams were too strong to forget
a previous summer. And what did it matter
that the excitement and boredom were both states
to be escaped except a grey   lost   and on
these mornings a ship would sink below the horizon
and winter covered the islands   a deserted beach

3

Once it was simpler, but in those
days people rarely left the city
It was quite enough to stand on the
    shingle bank when the tide was out
and the sun was setting and workmen
would lean forward to switch on television sets.

4

on winter evenings I would come across her by accident
standing in bookshops –
she would be staring into space dreaming
of – that I never knew

And most of this is far from true –
you know – we know so little
even on this trite level – but he – he was
more beautiful than any river

and I am cruel to myself because
of this and the indulgence it involves.

I loved him and I loved her
and no understanding was offered
to the first citizen
when the ricks were burnt.

The White Room

The book

1

It is so much a question of isolation and machines
and the systems never quite work out
and we're glad of it   or half-glad
through fear   the confusions when faced with 'logic'

'the nervous touch of sickly women'

and the motorcyclist started his machine and
putting the bike into gear left
and rode fast along the big highway
that led in a hard inflexible line to the
dock gates   drunken captains finally
sobering and breaking down with real tears
in the mahogany ward-room
while the chintz curtains were drawn by a fresh breeze
through an open port-hole and the heavy brass
catch glistened in the sunlight

'you're not fooling me or anyone else'

2

The 5.25 Pullman train, painted chocolate and cream, or
rather, nigger brown and cream, left Brighton station
on time as usual. It was October and dusk was just falling.
Autumn had taken the countryside and produced the
classic scene of woodlands whose leaves
slowly turned yellow.

The spire of the village church could
be seen behind the hill but we
had to hurry and so couldn't stop
this time. She drove the car
as fast as she could in silence
purposefully ignoring me. I
would have liked to have seen that
particular church – early Norman
has an innocence of its own.
It was the brown of the ploughed
fields, with rooks in the elms
and seagulls following the tractor,
it was . . .   No, you can't see
and the . . .   my contempt was equal
being a city-dweller by nature

3

the churchman was still leafing through his sermon
   notes when the tea was brought, and even this
did not wholly distract him.

I sat opposite him trying to read your book
and, really, your poems have never had a better setting
than this. The staff of the restaurant car were
discreet in the extreme. Their activities as
   expected went unnoticed. Things went
   accordingly and no real upset was allowed.

Our separation seemed only temporary

The main door was locked on that afternoon
but we were still able to walk round the churchyard
examining the inscriptions on the tombs. Later it rained.

I put down the book and carefully poured another cup of tea
avoiding spilling any
as on this section the track was very uneven
and the carriage rocked a great deal
The churchman was not so successful
but his minor irritation was only passing
I couldn't help but love him for this
and it seemed a reflection of my love for you
with your words still so close to me

The woodland outside at last disappeared
and then there was only the blackness broken
by the occasional orange light from a farm window

4

It was not the same and when the end was realized
with all its implications   I had grown calm

We had both avoided the logical sequence and were
glad of a breakdown in negotiations   The rest
would be taken care of ——
imagined loves and the riverside farewells
are only left for our weaker moments
the tears and longing were real enough until
a corner was rounded to meet a new distraction

We parted at 1st Avenue and 51st Street – it was July.
Wearing a cream-coloured suit and dark glasses
he crossed the street and then turned to wave – twice –
the lunch-time traffic was very heavy and I soon
lost sight of him.

His July return
for Larry Fagin

'rushing to embrace we were
at last in each others arms
I kissed his ear
and the sun reflected in my
gold ring making it glow even more
as I gripped his wrist
I saw how much darker my hand
was than his
but with our arms round each others shoulders
there was no question of inequality

The public buildings sparkled white
and the green of the park could be touched'

When I had finished writing this, I looked at
my watch. It was 2.30 in the morning.
I decided to go to bed. The rain had
stopped and I could see, when I parted
the curtain, that the streets were completely
deserted.
Tomorrow tourists would ride in small pleasure boats
down the river. I would be at work.
But it is still worth considering what this
means to both of us, if anything,
though both our meeting and this poem
are not free from a note of triviality

I wish I had a cat

Pastoral

Hell's Kitchen

'Today autumn was especially beautiful
the sun shone and bright leaves lay
happy on the pavement.

'I don't question this, and my reward
of pleasure is duly given — just as
the triple rainbow came so a
small girl called Celeste could see it.

'She too deserved what she got —
sooner or later we deserve what we get
and all our patience is rewarded.

'Celeste and her father left the bookshop
without any books. They needed none
in *this* world that I'm making now.

'I have to work in the bookshop
but long ago I stopped reading books.

'Instead I wait for the autumn sunshine
and the pale city square drunk with
its own lushness and the scent of dying leaves.

'And in this world I can put many other
people I love, besides Celeste and her father;
so the bookshop and square are really quite full.

'This all lasts until spring
when everything has to be changed,
but I can wait and spring has its own surprises.

'Summer of course follows. There is no
winter in my world.

'Perhaps as you read this poem
you will be pleased, and the smile of
memories and hopes will come into your face.

'I do hope this happens as it's the first
time I've written nature poetry.'

The separation

The time came when the desire to return
grew so strong that certain songs would automatically produce
the physical pain of real longing
just because they were markers of former street-days

the restraint was hard to bear
when the cold closed in for the year

when the thaw might come was a speculation
too distant to have much reality

The orchestra would come and go
and there seemed no regulation by which
one could plot or know their movements
yet at each appearance they never failed to chill
me with their blank faces and uncompromising playing
It was as though 'I' wasn't there,
as though it was all a self-supporting film
The leader of the orchestra would advance
towards me yet his eyes were set beyond me
It was so unbearable that I was forced to stay –
though the pleasure of mute acceptance was denied me
– their movements settled this
Many days were passed waiting in suspense for the next
appearance

When the sun shone you could see the cliffs
and seashore across
The little boats bobbed in the harbour

That the pain was doubly hard to bear since
it involved such self-restraint as to
not gulp down the remedy which was
a bottle with 'answer' crudely printed on the label –
the symbolism of this almost went too far

If a ticket was bought it could only mean one thing
and there waiting on the other shore
was a table loaded down with childish treats
and lots of cuddly bears romped all round the table
I had almost packed my knapsack
before I realized the spell-might break

I had tooted the car-horn for almost half an hour
outside their new house before I realized
    they might not want to come out

The old photo had faded and was now very worn
It was more than a matter of mere recognition

Yet underneath the forest even when the glacier
threatened imminent extinction
the desire to return to a warmer land
was as fierce as ever and no dangers
even in the form of pawnshop windows that displayed
neat rows of pistols and automatics – each with its neat blue
price tag hanging down so prettily – could deter me

It was a necessity to be continually reckoned with
even at the height of ecstasies;
The ice-cold chewed deeper
It hurt when the 'answer' was realized
and the whole camp stood silent for a minute

'How I love you . . .'

1

the fountain played long into the night
'how I love you . . .'
the house backed on to a large courtyard
which was filled with trees, plants, and
flowers in profusion. Wistaria climbed all the walls
and covered all the balconies, producing an atmosphere of
  unreality that

In a park a long way downtown the chess-players finally
put the pieces into the yellow box –
the box had a sliding lid on it –
This only left the drummers
but it is hard to know if they count
or if anything counts in these terms
when the basic qualities are still unknown
perhaps a comparison with a mountain landscape
with wild honeysuckle – perhaps – and boulders scattered

2

Riding back across the continent
just to lay beside the fountain again
my boots well worn by now and listening alone to
rock'n'roll on the radio usually saddens me
horses will have to be changed soon
but there are other things that won't

3

The night had passed and morning found us lying
naked in a large white room. Lifting a corner
of the blinds, it was noticed
that geraniums flowered and the fountain
still played surrounded by greenery.
On the opposite side of the courtyard a famous painter is
    known to live.
But her body, most of all, contained the infinite
in tenderness and wonder

4

The town became so tempting that I could easily
have stayed and forgotten forever that I had
come there as a stranger.
Yet more beautiful towns had known stagnation,
a series of pointless acts, a complete wrong-headedness
that was only to later be realized with regret.
There were plans of sorts – or rather –
the time had come when I knew
what a love meant and must be.

The courtyard may or may not exist,
yet fountains and greenery will always be there
when our bodies meet. Beneath her eyelids
the bright red of geraniums, and the wistaria's
blue flower in her breasts' delicate veins.

The Journey

1

I left Taos early in the morning – the sun was
rising and the first indians were entering the town.
I could leave now – I knew that Kit lay at rest
with all the peace a man can expect.

It was strange – getting used to the rhythm of my
saddle again after the long period of inactivity.
The hard stained leather when carelessly touched
burnt the fingers. Of course, I remembered other
towns, and was half afraid of the planned journey.
An expedition . . .

Tucson *was* hot *and* dusty. The arid mountains looked
on impassively. I found out the truth of the 1871
Apache atrocities when I read the farmer's accounts.
No holds were barred and the feats of cunning astonishing.

Riding across country – Fort Worth at last appeared
a low silhouette on the plain.

My death was near, but I had to find . . .
My love was left behind in the quiet sea town, and
I knew I would never return – and if at all, not for
many years to come, and this is a long time in which
memories can be completely lost. 'Tucson was inevitable'
and now Fort Worth had its own answers.

As I passed through the outskirts of the town I let
the reins lie slack, leaving the horse to walk at
the pace it chose, and enter the town as she willed.
When we turned into Main Street the body of a
recently lynched bandit was still sat in a chair on
the boardwalk. Flies crowded and crawled through his
beard and around his eyes. I could see the town had
still kept its sense of humour, despite the continual
threats. He was still wearing his hat and pistol.

I dismounted and according to the local law, checked
my rifle and pistols in at the sheriff's office. He
was a pleasant man, and we talked for a while. In
our conversation, we discovered that we both came
from the same town, and I took note of this as such
a bond could well be of use in the near future. I
decided to cultivate this friendship if I could,
despite his aloof nature.

All this travelling wearied me, and it seemed far
from its end. How was I to know?
But it was when entering the livery stables that I
realized who had passed me in the street only minutes
before. The realization and the shock at being so close
– at last – to a finality. But was it that final?

Many resolutions had been made in the past and within
months had been allowed to quietly melt away
in the back of my skull.

Would I be able this time to see it through?

2

Adjusting the long tight cuff on his blue shirt –
'Parting and travelling both include equal measures
of fear and joy.'

(That statement is so firm that it is almost final,
but really it doesn't mean much. What does matter
is that I am frightened. 'He is frightened' – these
words? their very inadequacy yet finality only leads
this problem further.

And – to be quite 'Honest', is it worth any effort?

I could leave now – the desert is still there. Sage
bush scratches the road's hot back when a wind is willing.
There *is* a real feeling of sureness when pulling
tight and buckling the wide strap beneath a horse's
belly, and the final act of parting is the last tug
on the saddle-horn to make sure all is secure.
But whether this mood goes beyond the town's outskirts
is another matter.

The line between escape and pursuit is so covered in
ground mist.)

Once in the mountains, I dismounted, secured the reins
to a stunted tree, and sat down on a boulder, and cried
– for no special reason. And this made my tears all
the more violent. I don't often cry, and when I do it's
always when alone.

One's own indulgences are not for strangers.

3

The stranger had passed me. Though, was it him? –
certainly I heard stones clattering under a horse's
hooves nearby in the night. But the small fire I had
built in the rocky hollow only produced enough light
for the most basic domestic activities.

Imagination can lead anywhere, and this can be another
cause of grief.

How long will we be dodging each other. Long ago the
distinction between pursuer and pursued was lost. We
were both chasing and fleeing from one another. The
whole affair became a matter of style. At times I
wonder if he really exists. Unreasonable accidents
can so easily be taken as proof, when desperation is
there, or lack of desperation.

The journey involved no symbols or allegory. It was
real enough. The story went on . . .

The mountains were by now blue smudges on the horizon,
and any discomfort felt just had to be borne. 'You're
not back east now.'

It would be many weeks before we reached Cheyenne.

4

To hide was necessary
and many grottoes existed in that region
when they came the citizens greeted them warily
and with a reservation that at first could not be understood
except by a few – later in the day
a building was seen in the middle of the plain
Many old men were driven out

I rode by

I couldn't tell them

Come now, let us walk in the garden
It was a mild evening
based on very little experience

Really there were few emotions involved in the telling
just as the final meeting was one in which
the departing could only smile and continue to watch the
river while the one who had to stay in that city
grew more agitated talking in a way he had
never done before and this was a pity

Yet when the time came and I was at last slowly riding
down Main Street I turned in my saddle and looked back
he was walking back across the street
into his office
'We both waved'

Still in the mountains I could see the road
stretch out before me for many miles
It would be three days crossing the desert
and then again the mountains which were now
just a blue smudge on the horizon

5

Many boats on that shore were already too rotten
to ever float again. The village had lain in neglect
for too many years. There was nothing for it. He
would have to wait there till the ferry was service-
able again, and that would not be for two days.

He spent the time mostly lying in his room. The
sun slanted across the white walls. At meal-times
he would rise from his bed and walk slowly into the
cantina, return to his room when he had finished
eating, or walk down to the stone jetty to see how
the work was progressing. One of the villagers would
stop hammering, look up at him, and wave.

It was a time when boredom could almost make him
give up the chase, and return – to where, he was
not even sure, but self-disgust and despair always
are homeless. It would merely be a change in his direction

What remained was the weight of his pistol as it
rubbed his thigh. He never took it off by day, and
at night he slept with the whole gun-belt at his
shoulder.

So many precious things had been lost; and what now?

In the evening he stood on the outskirts of the town.
The blood red sun was now resting on the horizon, and
the sky reared up in strata of white, yellow, blue
and purple. At such a time it would be very easy to
give way to tears.

The perfect gunman had to be met, set down and passed
through

6

Several months later I saw him, and for the first
time he saw me. It was almost too sudden for us
both. By this time we had grown clumsy. The years
of preparation and pursuit had wasted the earlier
tensions and energy. We just stood looking dumbly
at one another. All our resolutions were frozen.
If we had been able to move our hands, our fingers
would have been too clumsy to even get a pistol
from its holster. At last I reached for my gun,
but it was useless, like I said.
Trying to speak – that too was hard – but after . . .
The shock was so great, and the answer almost too easy.

Yet, finally, we agreed that evening to settle it,
to shoot it out standing six paces apart.

The evening came, and we both were now ready. The
delay had been necessary. We paced out the distance
and took up our set positions.

The only sound was that of the night birds preparing
for their evening's hunting.

The tractors are waiting

in the pain of silence
the meadows . . .
and from the barn's top loft
but nothing rustled among the bales of straw
the tractor is waiting in the meadow
but flowers arranged in a vase are no real comfort
    despite their scent

if an obsession were carried to its limit
then there would be a clean sky across
which grey clouds lovingly – and a lone
farmhouse stands out on the flat horizon
its plank walls bleached and the wheat
coarse and hard

The Argentine

1

Of course I was discontent with the ranch
the pampas was only there for one purpose
that the whole land knew of

The green continent groaned and stretched
while its brown rivers charged round in all directions
only to settle down as before
when the land fell asleep again

A single tree dominated the mountain top
but went no further than that

So many wrong and arrogant statements were
made in the geography books – and I
was not alone in resenting these

Brown chaos charged the towns and finally
smashed through into the very heart
of the people – they were terrified and some of
the people died too

'Can't you understand my difficulties?' was
whispered as I put my ear to the ground
'I wasn't prepared, and she could not wait
for ever'   the voice went on and on
with an endless story

I kicked every door down in the house
but found no one
It was opportune that at this moment

the group of horsemen galloped into
the court-yard. I had seen them at this
same time last year – but this time
I was prepared to ride away with them.

2

This was not the first migration
nor would this country be in anyway final –
the movement had been an agony dragged across
many lands   it was a well known process

The dead and numbed tundra or the sleepy estuary
with its brown banks and heavy jungle
'The grass was always greener on the other side'

She understood, I thought, that the ritual was grotesque
as it was necessary – and all this belonged elsewhere
just as the real love was elsewhere, but
this through accident and not desire

3

'He never visited the ranch' – and so in isolation
I continued as best I could. No profits were made
but neither were there any losses to talk of
What made it bearable was the memory – and hope –
an airport lounge with its automatic clock
and the milling crowds at the bus terminal . . .
He had a way of looking across a dinner table
– it at once commanded and yet asked for kindness.
Love and tenderness were the dominants – and the ceremony
of social acts was all that separated a fulfilment.
In fact pleasure was gained by the very anticipation,
by the polite dinner conversations and the easy talk
in the bars afterwards
The brief touch of his hand
or the caress of legs under a table
gave more than any previous experience

When these memories grew unbearable . . .
The mountains   the long ride and brief visits to other
    ranches
where nervousness made an evening pass quickly enough
in a series of laborious politenesses

On the way home, rain beating on the car roof
the essential notation of details like
the car's head-lamps and the night – their effect on one
    another
All this seized in weak desperation to distract
a realization, and sometimes even a regret

Such an image had been set so deep in my heart
that its destruction would inevitably cause
much more than local damage
and the fire chief didn't exaggerate when he said
'keep all those people well clear. That building's
going to collapse any minute.
It's little more than a burnt-out shell'

4

How could the two see reality as far as it meant
the truth of their situation or rather how true
were their words and sensations – both come and go
quite rapidly after all.

On the sidewalk in Fifth Avenue just below 12th Street
3 men were parting outside a German restaurant.
The older one had to go uptown – it was late –
and the 2 young men were
separately going to drift round the Village for a few hours
Then, as the taxi arrived, Joe reached up
and kissed John on the forehead.
The 3 split up. It was a hot june night – of course.

The second young man left outside this action
evidently felt something
It would seem that he was really the more concerned

with the older man and that he now regretted
his passiveness in that street, but he had had a reason
– though now it seemed a mistaken one.
He had feared to embarrass, where in fact a spontaneous
   act . . .

The frustration at a missed chance is universal
and a slight jealousy of the successful equally common
There were other days, and usually the older and the younger
   man
succeeded in gaining some degree of harmony

But . . .
the pressure of a train and a plane schedule
put a simple end to that development

Finding a torn letter left in a hotel room
he read – 'she must have felt something for me,
but I was torn in two,
and in the end I just waited for her to come to me
– and this got me nowhere, as she too had her fears
and I was not the only answer in that town.'

5

Mist rose from the marshes
and the rider was forced to skirt the estuary
and keep to the higher ground. Dew was heavy on
the coarse grass. The grazing lands stretched as far
as the eye could see in all directions.
And above this vast open countryside rose a hot sun
that soon thrust the mist back into the ground.

The cocks crowed and the horses grew restless
for the coming day's work. The dogs barked
and strained at their leashes as the first men
fed and watered the horses. This was the beginning . . .
Then midday.   Evening time   the faint sound of voices
from the other side of the yard

6

The rare view from the mountain pass
suddenly made everything seem clear
and the whole geography somehow too simple
The answers were obvious and the route through
all the country ahead

The journey had to be made and the horsemen were right
But the weight of possessions held on to,
if not for love of them, then for some sense of duty
and fear

These accounts of past and future journeys
became boring . . . and any violence that might have been
has now grown limp like the vase of dead flowers
that the efficient house-keeper will surely clear away

White

for Tom Clark

It all began so softly and white was the
colour that showed the most dominance
In fact – it was a glorious white
This meant that the toy soldiers had to all be rearranged;
confusion on all levels and 'no one was really prepared'
My arms were no longer tired – the rest had been good

It was a happy occasion
but you were so surprised to see the same flags still hanging
limply from the long balcony of the state apartments
In the end the ritual remains unaltered
and that too is comforting and like the 'last words'
of an important general's speech
talking of history, religion and tradition

The only sabotage was the irritating acts of open vanity
performed by women consciously or unconsciously

The paintings would have to be winter landscapes
and this means lots of white paint –
I've bought it for you already. he said 'look in that cupboard'

The New Start is near
and white is so tender anyway
like the little sail-boat in the large round pond

The doomed fleet

1

the entire palace was deserted, just as was
the city, and all the villages along the 50 mile
route from the seaport to the capital.
It was not caused by famine or war –
'It was all my fault.'

The troops of desperate cavalry were ridiculous.
The naval guns could pick off
whatsoever their whim dictated,
but there was only one commander-in-chief.

2

The grey battleships lay in silence
anchored in the middle of the harbour.
They were ready all the time –
the only necessity in all this was decisions.
That may appear laughable – it's all
so simple.

The wounded was a subject never touched on
in the officers' mess. And the question of
occasional small but brutal outbreaks of
disease was similarly treated.

Nothing that could disturb the carefully planned
vanity was tolerated. That was the new order.

3

Grey waves slapped against the sides of
the iron grey battleships. Seabirds screeched
above the wind; they don't sing.
Even the ships appeared deserted, except
for the occasional dark figures that would
hurry along a deck and then disappear
through a hatch-way as abruptly as when they first
appeared. It was their continual menace,
however, that undeniably asserted their presence.

The menace. The power that vibrated
from the ships. The grey harbour.
Power. Menace. All terminals irrelevant.

In such a setting, it is not surprising
that tears or tenderness, shown by a small
but delicate gesture or caress, were of no consequence.

The men's minds were set –
they didn't understand 'pity'. The very word
had been deliberately deleted from all the books
scattered among the fleet. They needn't have feared.

4

With so few exits left . . .
'That was really ridiculous, wasn't it?'
Murder was just one of the expected events.
It would be carried out with the precision
of any naval operation and with the coldness.
Everyone knew their place and to disrupt the
series would be not so much reprehensible
as an admission of bad breeding in the extreme.

It was only actual closeness to the event
that allowed any levity. The midshipmen were
only boys, after all. And the officers and the men . . . ?
– who is ever free from the fears and shadows
so firmly established in every childhood?

The point of 'safe return' had long since been passed.
There were no maps in existence
for this ocean, nor were there any charts
of seas, harbours or sheltered estuaries
where the least clue or news-item
might be found concerning 'The Successful Voyage'.

Maybe they never did get there and, instead,
the whole expedition lay at the bottom.
This already begins to sound like a very bad boy's story.

5

Age began to show . . . and the divisions widen
and become even more resolute and rigid.
'What could have been' became altogether another story
like the family photos in the captain's wallet
– there was no room for sentimentality now.

The heavy service revolver seemed somehow too
melodramatic to be real enough for its purpose.
I suppose there was no doubt about efficiency
– only about motives. Wasn't this word
'melodramatic' something of a key?
How *real* was the death to be?
Was it an act of necessity or escape, or
one last weak self-justification, self-gratification . . . ?
The scene was, apart from superficial changes,
only too familiar, and tired.
The unwilling audience would at least be glad
of the concrete finality of this latest show.
It couldn't have much of a sequel, thank God.

The chart table was cluttered with empty coffee cups
and a haze of cigarette smoke filled the navigator's cabin.
It was very late at night, and the navigator
had fallen asleep, fully clothed and exhausted.
But even now, with so much unanswered and so much
    confusion,
there was in the atmosphere a feeling of finality

whose very grimness brought a strange joy
and relief. The death would not be that dark –
The dead body somehow would know a sweetness
that can be compared to the parable of the
bees' honey inside the dead lion's carcass.

The fleet steamed out beyond the point.
Nothing was free from the ridiculous and 'pain'.
The laughter was not disrespectful,
nor was it really that inappropriate.
The night sky was a dark blue and most stars visible.
Salt waves broke over the rusted iron decks.

'Goodbye Tom'

The dull mist that . . . the castle stands still
within its moat   'Wild One'
and the sadness leads the same way when facilities
are there   the work of their provisions

The radio plays more music, though it is the
soldiers in the castle who select the dance records
and the nature of the provisions is still a secret
The whole network was clearly set out on the wall chart
by the use of brightly coloured pins and narrow red ribbons
that linked certain points – but the next morning
all that remained was a faded wall

and the 'dull mist' – what became of that?
It could always be put down as an omen or, even
more disturbing, as a symbol
of the approaching dream that marked the couple
for life.

No pity need have been wasted on the castle
its walls were beyond all hope of restoration
The people really were glad and the tourists sighed . . .
with relief the Wild One and the provisions
were destroyed and so was the confusion and the sadness
The number of loose ends to be tied and tidied
also were destroyed – everything was destroyed –
until the orgy of destruction itself became ludicrous and
    upsetting

When the site was at last at peace
there was only 'the dull mist' left
What else happened was forgotten

'You will soon lose sight of me
sleeping or awake. It is too much to expect.
Goodbye – '

          It is all as though the whole
land decided upon this, that 'the tribe
should once more be scattered'
The words when printed in a text book grew
as cold and distant from events as the
illustrations of traditional tribal tattoos
whose magic and power . . .

'Are they scattered?'
'That was a stupid question, sir.'
The dull mist parted by the approaching dream
like a new plough-share slicing the air
and black earth   Soldiers playing cymbals
The Words were left there singing 'Keep on Babylon'

Plato was right though

for Ed Dorn

1

The empty house – the empty country – the empty sky.
Reverse it to A – B – C.

A: The large house
filled with many people – servants and guests –
it is now a country mansion.
It is white and has extensive grounds and woods.
There are many people.
They hunt and shoot. They laugh and talk.
In the evenings they play games.
It is all like a picture-book
that teaches vocabulary to foreigners –
each different object in the picture is numbered,
and below is the list of words that correspond
to the many numbers. So – 12 is table;
5: vase; 16: father . . . and so on.

B: The full country.
The map blocked out with the red of cities
– that's the agreed colour in the atlas key.
This continues into the 3rd dimension with
'concrete and neon' parodying themselves.
Countries, armies, 'The People' struggling with
'The People'. The borders on the map look
so pretty, with dotted lines in bright coloured inks
– all yellows and reds – dot dot dot – and in practice

nothing more glorious than a stretch of
ill-kept road with a line of battered poplars
one side and strands of barbed wire on the other.
The bad spy story continues . . . The plot is very obvious
and stupid, even if it *is* all true.
No one could look at this and take it seriously.
And it wasn't just that the generals and borders
were ridiculous, but that the whole situation,
– including the very existence of the cities –
was wholly laughable.
The atlas became the one truly funny book,
and it did not escape our notice that what was portrayed
should be regarded in the same light,
To be totally 'negative' in believing the
countries as they were (and the cities) were
painfully absurd and grotesque seemed
perhaps the saner and more realistic.
It was a very pompous speech . . .

C: The sky was crowded with airplanes of all colours –
a totally unreal picture with dozens of
happy red, blue, orange and green
airplanes filling the sky in a mechanical
rainbow. Each plane painted entirely in its
colour with no other markings, flies through a series
of aerobatic stunts, diving climbing,
rolling over and over, and 'looping the loop'.
This is happening in a clear blue summer sky –
there has been no trace of a cloud all day.

2

All the previous locations are now impossible.
There is only this confusion in which no one
knows exactly what is going on.
The planes or the hesitating crowd on the lawns,
the house party going its usual way –
but this only in a vacuum.
Outside is total darkness

dominated by the sure knowledge of Death
that takes on an almost human persona
and vibrates like the engines of an ocean liner at night
that can be felt many miles away and yet never seen.
(Black, as you know, is the negation of colour
and strictly it is not even a colour,
while White is all colours.)
And white is the love and only light that can be seen
to really exist besides the blackness.
The White is the only sure and real force
in an otherwise brutal chaos, and the only
home when all else has been lost.
(This new 'simplicity' was, in fact, a blessing
and advantage never before possessed, and that now
made the struggle easier and brought a sure relief
in the victory that before was confined to day-dreams.)
A lone parachutist drifting down through the blue . . .
And even if he *is* shot dead in his harness
by the border guards, who really cares?
He has the same chances as anyone else.
'When you're facing death or junk, you're always on your
    own,
and that's exactly how it is,' he said. It became daily
more obvious that such clichéd truisms were only too true.

It is not a question of doubts or a lack of faith
in the forces of Good . . . but from this black and white
landscape, what is it that will finally be launched?
There is an obvious and reasonable impatience
at the slowness of the expedition to set out and,
at least, attempt an exploration . . . an examination
of what had happened in the past and what
could come out of the Interior afterwards.

3

The fact that there should be this co-existence
of opposites . . . A desert, a barren plain, or,
to reduce this to its basic elements, a complete emptiness and
    darkness,

– faced by a crowded world of absurd objects
and events, and a tangled 'confusion'; and this portrayed
quite clearly in a desperate heaping-up of words
and pictures. The brightly coloured airplanes flying low
and at great speed over the countryside and approaching the
    towns
brought a wave of 'cold fear' upon all who saw them,
that the jollity of the planes' appearance at first denied.

It was this fact, above all, that was finally realized –
and no matter how painful the realization, it had to be
    accepted
that what had gone on too long was due entirely
to a mental laziness that could live with this 'co-existence'.
There was no expedition to be expected or any news
of it to be eagerly awaited. If anything
was to be found or gained it would only come through
a 'personal action'.
                    'All the necessary equipment was there.
I had only to dress and begin.
And it was not a matter of fierce lions from the story-book,
or navigating my sampan through a wild and thundering
    gorge
only to have to fight 300 Chinese rebels the other side
single-handed with only a revolver and my walking stick.
The fun of these jaunts was a thing of the past.
What it meant now was to live like anyone else
– getting up in the morning, washing, eating meals . . .'

The convalescence, though once necessary,
was now over. All the wounds had healed and
the neat white scars could only be mementos.
This left no real excuses or causes for further delay.
'And the one simple and basic fact that love
had become a supreme power that radiated from me
was now the key to everything. And no matter how much
time would be needed, the struggle to deal with this
and other pressures was there and only waited to be
used. Like the quiet in the ship's engine-room,
this inactivity seemed wrong.'

For some reason the word 'LOVE' does not suggest
a strength, or grace, only a mild ineffectuality.
Yet beyond the romantic charades and the gaudy neon letters
outside the theatre – when the Real, and
the True essence is gained (or found), it's only this
love that creates a joy and happiness able to finally
dismiss a cruel haunting by Death, and meet the 'world'.
And what the words and poems attempt degenerates into this –
a clumsy manifesto in which the words used
appear emptier than ever before and the atmosphere
more that of an intense but bad Sunday School.
————————————————PLATO was right to banish
poets from the Republic. Once they try to go beyond the
colours and shapes, they only ever fail, miserably –
some more gracefully than others.

Landscapes

The paint box

What did you do? We all know how tired
you were, but you did, didn't you?
I mean the formula can be turned most ways
and it's only a matter then of local colour
to give *that* touch of distinction.
The surface then appeared different –
but under the paint?
Canvas was universal – everywhere.
The tubes of paint were so fat
and funny, as they didn't matter so much.
It was 'the rose mist floating down
on the white mountain crags'
that was in everyone's mind.
The poem was printed out like a neat label
and stuck below the picture.
We've been here before, haven't we?
Yes! And it's now one more poem.
That's funny, isn't it? or maybe
it's not so funny, but scary instead.
I mean the whole routine of bare
canvas and the paints all squeezed out
on the palette and then it's just for someone
to step out and say 'GO' in a loud voice.
And the day goes by in slapping noises
as more and more paint is used up.

When the geography was fixed

for Marian

The distant hills are seen from the windows.
It is a quiet room, and the house is in a town
far from the capital.
The south-west province even now in spring
is warmer than the summer of the north.
The hills are set in their distance
from the town and that is where they'll stay.
At this time the colours are hard to name
since a whiteness infiltrates everything.
It could be dusk.
The memory and sound of chantings
is not so far away – it is only a matter
of the degree of veneer at that moment.
This is not always obvious and for many
undiscovered while their rhythm remains static.
It's all quite simple,
once past the door – and that's only a figure
of speech that's as clumsy as most symbols.
This formality is just a cover.

The hills and the room are both in
the white. The colours are here
inside us, I suppose. There's still a tower
on the skyline and it's getting more obscure.
When I say 'I love you' – that means
something. And what's in the past
I don't know anymore – it was all ice-skating.
In the water a thick red cloud
unfurls upwards; at times it's almost orange.

A thin thread links something and there are
fingers and objects of superstition
seriously involved in this.

The canvas is so bare
that it hardly exists – though the painting
is quite ready for the gallery opening.
The clear droplets of water sparkle
and the orange-red cloud hangs quite seductively.

There is only one woman in the gallery now
who knows what's really happening on the canvas –
but she knew that already, and she
also instinctively avoided all explanations.
She liked the picture and somehow the delicate
hues of her complexion were reflected in it.
She was very beautiful and it soon became
obvious to everyone that the whole show
was only put on to praise her beauty.
Each painting would catch one of the colours
to be found in her skin and then play with it.
Though some critics found this delicacy
too precious a conceit, the landscape
was undeniable in its firmness
and the power that vibrated from the
colours chosen and used so carefully.

During the whole gallery-opening a record of primitive red
indian chants was played – and this music
seemed to come from the very distant hills
seen in every painting – their distance was
no longer fixed and they came nearer.
But recognitions only came when all
the veneer was stripped off
and the inexplicable accepted in the whiteness.

The house

The rain over the hills – the shades of blue and grey
in the clouds on the horizon with evening coming –
The house is on the outskirts of the town;
and the view is something unknown in the capital
and these colours in the clouds are meaningless there.
It is different – a horizon which is formed by
a line of green hills and a solitary tower.
It's all like the early landscape in the city gallery.
And this question of painting and vision
and which seems the more real is fascinating –
I can't explain this. But beyond the hills
are the moors.
The brown and green in the hills shows
there is a forest up there.
This is getting mysterious, and the tower
is certainly not free from a magic awe.
The rain is so good and soon it will be night.
The clouds have almost gone and the sky
is taking on a pink colour.
It's as though time really has ceased, and
all I have to do is watch the bird
I disturbed by the river fly off through
the trees. The river has many eddies
and I can stand by the weir fascinated
for a long time – but I must return
to the house with its view of the hills.
Time really has ceased and
the simple mechanism of the revolver is stuck.

Sea coves

Sea coves and cliffs, the deserted beach –
they all mean so little
You are there and that is what it is
The clumsiness of my actions
We care for each other and love.
The sea is quiet and the streets
in the small port so narrow,
but somehow we get through.
It's only belief – what else
can words do? 'Love.'
This isn't a parable – the objects
are real enough, they have powers.
Allegories are in the past – there isn't
the luxury or time now.
This sounds brusque – what is the sound,
of our love? The words collapse again.
That was weak, wasn't it?

I can't get my paints out now.
It's not the time. You know –
we both collapse, but somehow
it's as superficial as the waves
and the whole seascape.
We're here and stay put.
It's our move; we paint what we like
and do what we like,
and all the words like 'somehow' and the
objects and the 'powers' are so little.
To talk of the plane now
would be unlucky – it's just there,

and the tarmac is so pretty with its oil slicks
and the orange wind-sock beside the white hangar.
'Yes, that sounds right, doesn't it?'
I do like oil slicks, but I love you.

The 'utopia'

The table was filled with many objects

The wild tribesmen in the hills,
whose very robes were decorated with designs
of a strangeness and upsetting beauty
that went much further than the richly coloured silks
embroidered there could ever suggest; . . .

There were piles of books, yet each one
was of a different size and binding.
The leathers were so finely dyed. The blues
and purples, contrasting with the deceptive simplicity
of the 'natural' tans.
And this prism and arrangement of colours
cannot be set down – the fresh arrangements
and angles possible can only point through a door
to the word 'infinite' made of white puffy clouds
floating high in a blue summer sky;
this has been written there by a small airplane
that is now returning to its green landing field.

The table is very old and made of fine mahogany
polished by generations of servants.
And through the windows the summer blue skies
and white clouds spelling a puffy word.
And on the table the books and examples
of embroidery of the wild hill tribesmen
and many large and small objects – all of which
could not help but rouse a curiosity.

There are at times people in this room
– some go to the table – things are moved –
but the atmosphere here is always that of quiet and calm
– no one could disturb this.
And though the people are the only real threat,
they are all too well trained and aware
to ever introduce the least clumsiness
or disturbing element into the room.

At times it is hard to believe
what is before one's eyes –
there is no answer to this except the room itself,
and maybe the white clouds seen through the window.

No one in the house was sure of the frontiers
and the beautiful atlas gilded and bound with blue silk
was only of antiquarian interest and quite useless
for the new questions. The whole situation
was like a painting within a painting and
that within another and so on and so on –
until everyone had lost sight of their original landmarks.
The heath melted into the sky on the horizon.
And the questions of definition and contrast
only brought on a series of fruitless searches
and examinations that made everyone irritable and exhausted.

Once the surveyors had abandoned their project
the objects once more took over.
It would be false to deny the sigh of relief
there was when this happened and calm returned.

The bus bumped down the avenue
and ahead were the mountains and the woods
that burst into flower as spring settled.
The plan and the heavy revolver were all quite in keeping
with this, despite the apparent superficial
difference and clash of worlds –
there was really only one world.
It wasn't easy – admittedly – and someone
had to stay behind and . . .

The word in the sky had slowly dissolved
and was now nowhere to be seen.
But instead the sun was flooding the whole room
and everything took on a golden aura
– this meant we were even aware of the
band of horsemen now riding through the forest
that surrounded the valley.

The many details may appear evasive
but the purpose of the total was obvious
and uncompromising

The final painting

The white cloud passed over the land
there is sea always round the land
the sky is blue always above the cloud
the cloud in the blue continues to move
– nothing is limited by the canvas or frame –
the white cloud can be pictured like any
other clouds or like a fist of wool
or a white fur rose
The white cloud passes a shadow across
the landscape and so there is a passing greyness
The grey and the white both envelop
the watcher until he too is drawn into the picture
It is all a journey from a room through a door
down stairs and out into the street
The cloud could possess the house
The watchers have a mutual confidence
with the approaching string of white clouds
It is beyond spoken words what they are
silently mouthing to the sky
There was no mystery in this – only the firm
outline of people in overcoats on a hillside
and the line of clouds above them
The sky is blue The cloud white with touches
of grey – the rest – the landscape below –
can be left to the imagination
The whole painting quietly dissolved itself
into its surrounding clouds

Question of geography

Facing the house   the line of hills
across the valley   a river somewhere
hidden from view   the thickets there
I can't remember   the colours
green   a rich brown   as the sun shone
turned to slate grey   at times a soft blue smudge
with dusk or rain clouds   the details obscured
but like a long ridge setting the skyline
Months gone by   the seasons now almost full circle

It was spring and our garden was thick with
primroses
Each morning I would go out and . . .

Ridge in the distance   everything the same
as before   it must be
The moors edged with pine woods
in the south-west province   a repetition
but the cathedral town unchanged
It makes no difference who was there
all inevitably reduced to the question of
geography or memory

And now awaiting the next spring
set in yet another place   this too with
its own colours and forms
the others seeming somehow irrelevant in the present
   excitement
but still real like a very sure background
– you paint over the picture and start on
the new one   but all the same it's still there
beneath the fresh plains of colour

Central Park Zoo
for Marian

Looking at the zoo   the great white park
of a misty winter's afternoon   'you're great!
and I love you for it'
All the animals have their thick winter coats on
– the childish humour of this is so enjoyable –
A brass clock strikes the hour of three and
sets in motion mechanical chimes that are
beaten out by rampant bears and prancing monkeys
with heavy metal limbs jerking to the rhythm
– this obviously moves the crowd of children who're
watching – some laugh with 'joy', others gasp with 'wonder'

Let's call this charming story 'A day at the zoo' –
all essays to be handed in by the end of the week

But back to the winter and coats
It's very crisp today and the air is clear
The *buffaloes* are magnificent and beautiful – they are a rich
       brown, and the hair is not matted as it was in summer
       'alas'
A pair of *bob cats* lie with their front paws round each
       others necks – like lovers – they lick each others
       fur (in turn) – it is a golden yellow
A pair of *badgers*
A pair of *lynx*
Two pairs of *racoons*
and the *grizzlies and polar bears* lie sleeping in the sun

Let's call this 'The Peaceable Kingdom: A Painterly Reference'
or 'Winter in the Zoo' or 'A Day at the Zoo'
In fact let's forget what we'll call this
Instead let's . . .   returning to
the zoo in the corner of the park
the white mist hanging over the trees
The fact we can become children again
shows how right we were in
believing in our love despite the canyon
which we entered stumbling along the dark bed
of the Bad Water river
But we climbed out the other side
though taken by surprise on topping the rim
never having realized the end was so very near
But there it was – the herd of buffalo
grazing on the lush plains
Geography in our sense *is* exciting
Plotting the whole course now
Sunlight and the shadows of fast
moving clouds sliding across the grassland
I imagine North Texas   or even Dakota   Montana

'The end' only of this canyon   but a continuation
of something greater   compare it to a plateau
of great size and richness laced with gentle
deaths at its edges   the spirits of the tribe
waiting with a deep love for us
It's not so much of a descent either – but these
details can wait   you see

'You're great! and very wise' we laugh as
we reach the top of the rock outcrop
'and I love you for it'

We flower   we continue from where we left off before
though the statement of this can only be
something secondary for us and therefore decorative
There's no worry
                    'People of the World, relax!'
We walk among the animals
          the cages upset you

When I really think I know you're always right
there's no worry   we're on the same planet
and so very lucky
that the poem should end like this
is very good

Halos

I wait   the madonna slowly glides across a gold surface
the icon's doors half open   a trumpet   an angel's wing
'and Mohammed is His prophet'   beyond the blue sky's
   floating
even the pure patterns that stay free from any sin of imitation
You can understand   the magic of flowers
painted in a formal enough setting yet
the very radiance of these gathered flowers   the woodlands

Your strength   and 'independence'   the accompanying
   childishness
is admitted part of this   but
This mixture can only excite   you stand beside me
no one weighs or sucks the spirits in

The novelty can bring many dangers   a nakedness
among sword points   yet the alternative can only be
a disturbed sleep   the crossroad choice
'Sooner murder an infant in its cradle than nurse unacted
   desires'

At the third tree you begin again
a small pastel sketch by Redon
and after the vase of flowers some sort of silver –
or is it golden? – maybe – aura round your head

Telescope

The army advanced by night
at dawn the pearl grey of the sea
a large bird flying too slowly   I may be tired now
but lying in bed watching thin white clouds
passing through the window in a clear sky
Your smile is inside me   I wait
In this morning stillness everything seems at peace
the white sheets   the delicate ring of my watch
ticking in a bare white room overlooking the sea
One direction the harbour and the green band of waves
below the horizon – the other the heavy roundness
of the hills, the darker green of the Downs
The army subsides and melts like the night at dawn
– it's in the past now. Thoughts of you glow inside me.
A pale late winter sunshine floods the whole landscape
in a harsh white light and so makes it
look totally bare – the word 'naked' can even be used now –
and this same air of nakedness in the sunlight
is like an announcement of the coming spring
The comparison expands and I see this all as a
reflection of your coming return that I now wait for
and how I lie here this morning thinking of you
Far from the shore a small cargo boat presses on
– from here its progress looks painfully slow
but this doesn't matter   neither I nor the boat's crew
can be ruffled with such good things so obviously in store for
   us

New Zealand outback
for Marian

'The three horsemen' is written down in the book
You gave me the book   I love you
My great-grandfather, his brother and a friend
rode out and someone took their photo.
Snap.

It is Sunday and the scent of lilies
really floods the room. It is also a sultry afternoon
in summer.   I love you.
The picture-book is lying open on the table
and shows an engraving of a lily,
your poem about a lily and our love.

The three horsemen disappear over the horizon
I feel as confident as my great-grandfather
that I love you.
Snap.

Formal portrait

The Emperor Shah Jahan is shown in his garden
in a small portrait painted with tempera and gold
Soft green hollyhocks with pink flowers, a marigold,
daisies and small plants, and flowers so delicate
and whose names I don't yet know

Ladies sit delicately on the swings
hung among the trees under chosen branches heavy with cool
   shades
– quiet attendants pushing them to and fro;
the only noise in the garden
being the creak of the ropes and the birds' cries.
On such hot afternoons

One thing for certain, the princess must not be harmed
under any circumstances   Negotiations for this
are at this moment in progress   The guards have young
   faces

A mirror made of highly polished metal
I see your reflection in this and in myself
The moon shines too above the many seatowns strung along
   the coast
It is coloured a clear white cream
and dominates the entire night sky

In Kashmir and other Himalayan foothills
Bichitr the artist in '1633' came to see
you swim naked to the waist in 'a lotus pond' –
the hills behind the colour of a sliced blood-orange
I watch you undisturbed – your neat firm breasts.

The same lady is on a swing now
in a courtyard – steel grey storm-clouds gather
above the Kangra Valley
The same lady is caught in a storm as she hurries
through the woods – the snakes hurry for cover as well
'At the tryst' she stands below the orange flower tree
It is hard to know if these are exercises in grammar
or attempts at communication of sorts
either by the painter or the lady maybe
Sometimes you are the lady, but most often
you are even more beautiful than she is
or ever could be.
The long black hair and clear forehead
your dark brown eyes set between narrow lids

The number of possible scenes and descriptions
seems nearly as unlimited as the ever changing light

As you sleep the fine garden is deserted
except for the moon and a few tigers
The Emperor wears rich scarlet slippers
as he stands beside the hollyhocks unnoticed
Perhaps tonight he thinks of the war on the plains
or remembers when his palace was eaten by fire
You are quite safe and there is no worry

Tibet

Your temple music is fine
and there is such weight and ceremony in the actions
the swaying voices of faceless religious
Coming down the trail the yaks and behind them
the dazzling gold of the monastery roofs
high up the valley   When you fall silent
there's only the dark brown of your eyes – at dawn
I find flecks of green   Whatever it is . . .
the white rocks were very slippery
Chalk   Dark woods beside all this
In the distance vague lines of colour
caught by the sun   So many small bells
tinkling in the sunlight   the brass flashing
You are beyond this
Not in the desert though I am at fault
the morning only reveals further cruelties
after such richness   you are faced with
the coming night and a long trek across the plateau
where the darkness is cut by loud reports
from boulders cracking with the ice
Though I act as guide it is your light
that radiates from the sanctuary
I let you enter then wait outside
knowing what your return could mean
It is a matter of stripping these animal hides
from the walls of our hut and feeling their strength
once more

Return of the native

The clouds descend so warm and heavy   again
A rigid number gives time to the day but with no
certainty except the recognition of being here before
Once more facing   being engulfed even
'I never thought it would be this good'   and consequently
sway held up by a soft 'greyness'   is that it?
eyes narrowing and the lids growing heavy too

There is piping music in the tents   the horses?
Can the stories ever be told once too often?
a new freshness radiates from the change perhaps

Slowly the clouds thin and . . .

The horses to be seen grazing far across the grasslands
dead zebras lying in the deep grass
and in the distance the roar of surf pounding some coast-line

the giraffe is a bright gold

A wind flicking over the pages of this picture book
in which time seems to go backwards
'early lithography'   'pursued by furies'?
a volume bound in coarse blue cloth whose spine is so faded
the dust settling outlined against the shafts of sunlight
dividing the room
and all this despite various private emotions
whose relevance cuts only too deeply for those who . . .
looping-the-loop

'The tents have been cleared and there had been
no one there to leave even the simplest message with
So, starting from the very beginning again –
the menfolk sat round the fires examining their bodies for lice
and other parasites. Each success met with roars of approval.'
Closing the book

And on the return, after taking in the view from the window
once again, even praising its beauty,
yet all this more a formality than any fresh response –
an old lady's pilgrimage rather than JERUSALEM flashing

Reports continued to flood the warden's office –
throughout the entire district, on and off the Reservation,
carcasses of large and small game were being sighted
and in increasing numbers. The heavy clouds
no longer decorated the distant horizon – 'love you'
what does that mean? in God's name in the distance –
they filled the air like snow-drifts
a soft 'greyness'   where WHITE had dazzled

The picture-book's colours had so easily drugged us
with their richness that only the vague glow of the present
backed with irrelevant and totally unreal dates suggesting
    history
appeared to exist until an unexpected gap in the clouds
revealed the proof of rumours once so quickly dismissed
It was not a matter of the odd death by accident
but of a whole bloody trail stretching back into the distance –
beasts trampling in their panic   'Irrecoverable Damage'
totally inadequate if ever a 'judgement' – and the time
unrepeatable and lost beyond the plodding repetition of
    cruelties

With dawn approaching, the birds singing in the darkness
– a young woman talks in her sleep, then laughs –
a happiness even in her dreams

This year

The children playing on the front step
the sea is green
today   the power games
can't be gentler

The walk along the beach at night
shingle   back home the animals
all playing games underlined with violence
maybe cruelty

Everyone gets very religious
this year   it even opens out
but the desire to give out messages
has to be supressed in favour of

A neat square is moist and green
its trees each have their
thin black branches that glisten with water
found by accident   it's very warming

To be here   the sea is green
at times grey   there are two empty houses
in the neat square   the windows   a black enamel
Surprised

As she undresses   the children playing in the street
the sea is green   her young body womanly
loose clothes hid her great beauty
at times grey   'olive' she said

Everyone gets very religious
I can understand why   even the power games
gentler   when play stops
what then?   gentler   surprised

Undressed   it's very warming
her young breasts fuller than   no messages
in favour of   nor against
her nipples are small and a defeating pink

Today   green power games can be
gentler than the sea   on the beach
shoo the animals   your lap
her beauty undresses   the sea

Soft white

When the sea is as grey as her eyes
On these days for sure   the soft white
mist blown in from the ocean   the town dissolving
It all adds up   her bare shoulders

Nakedness   rolling in from the sea
on winter afternoons   a fine rain
looking down on the sand   and shingle
the waves breaking on the shore   and white

It is impossible to deny what
taken by surprise   then wonder
the many details of her body
to be held first now   then later

In body and mind   the fine rain outside
on winter afternoons   the nakedness
of her bare shoulders   as grey as her eyes
the sea rushing up the beach as white as

The whole outline called 'geography'
meeting at a set of erotic points
lips   shoulders   breasts   stomach
the town dissolves   Sex   Thighs   legs

Outside   then across her nakedness
it rains in the afternoon   then the wonder
her body so young and firm   dissolves the town
in winter   grey as her eyes

The cliff walk

In the distance   the cliff walk
decorated piers now antique   you lie away
the ocean is so vast   someday
I am waiting   is your patience enough?

Ghosts haunt the sites of our past
I   someday soon
across the ocean   coming
such love goes far beyond

Green seas look soft and turn grey
the white chalk   a cap of dark woods
it is a matter of wonder
and what comes with time?

Such hands   silhouetted in the window
with a sea coast stretching off into the distance
then maybe it falters   the window   in a white glow
such a blue sky   in all this

the cliff walk turning from side to side
and soft winds brushing   ghosts
distance of the sea-town
you filter the pine woods   there you . . .

green paint wet on the railings
your clothes will be marked

HMS Little Fox

Dawn of the monsters

The sky grows pale with dawn
the birds sing there – maybe only three or four distinct songs –
but with more clarity in this than anywhere else
At this hour the sky is a soft blur
with black silhouettes on the horizon and pale stars
scattered – no one caring if they do move

In a different town far from here . . .
I'm not sure why I should be aware of you
– a common 'wretchedness'?
more imagined than real?   You forgive me
there's nothing else to do   'I give in.'

Paleness soaks deeper and deeper into the atmosphere
like an admission of collapse where nothing is touched

Chemical days

'The fix' can only mean
the man with two blue flags who stands all day
on the cliff top. Now he's waving them at
the aircraft-carrier, HMS Blue Flag, that is
as hard and clumsy as most machines.
This process is called an 'euphemism'.
The wars, fathers, spacemen, soldiers –
just so many toys to be broken or dismembered.
Even the flag man and his strange obsession . . .
What there is . . .   I mean, couldn't it really be
a matter of compasses like fixing the sun or
the stars, or the hour for the 'fix'?
This process is called a 'smoke screen'.
When it's raining and the isolation of the day
can only mean 'the fix' or a studied chaos
of words and pictures in the hope of distraction
or, even weaker yet more honest, justification
for existence. Tears are so much of the past.
'Shall I have them all shot?
or just the leaders? That's quite a question.'
Click! went the heels. A door banged in the yard.
Blue flags fluttering – 'What's happening?'
It was all there waiting – a complete change of lives
– why the delay? Courage wasn't even
relevant, only 'common sense' for a change.
She was still waiting in the yard patiently.
Everyone acknowledged her beauty and love.
'this stupidity'

Dazzle

       the dazzle of the New
– its own great and unique beauty –
(her long black hair reflecting a summer morning)
like the fresh white liner at anchor
in the sparkling blue sound of this Pacific island

An equatorial republic asking for foreign aid –
the large ship at anchor; a new pipe-line
and harbour installations; the glossy black capstan
and tar melting on the roads.
So many excuses and subsequent apologies
for the numerous blunders and inefficiencies
of my native workers –
the covers and symbols of my own astonishment
and love for you

But still I can't stop this wonder
that dumbfounds me everytime I see you,
or, when alone, ever come to a full realization
of what's happened and is still happening
and will continue happening.

I just gape at you
and know how I must appear so crazy
all red faced and sweating in the ridiculous
general's uniform of my small republic.
I am weighed down with gold braid,
epaulettes, medals, swords and nonsense,
as you pass in a light summer dress.

Forestry work No. 1

Did I say that?
The prospect of such expanses still to be covered . . .
hardly having set out   intimidated   so soon?
Up onto the ridge   the forest here like a cool grove of ash
with sunlight filtering down
Like a pilgrimage, maybe?
On the map there are a series of points   'The Procession'
Later playing with the children, it's quite natural . . .
Your body gives   'The Acceptance'

I pick the wild flowers carefully
and take exactly one example of each species
'and with reeds and yellow marsh flowers in the clearing'
this   conscious   and   essential   'delicacy'   in   handling
   surroundings,
of course, flows out   takes in the
You understand this when we touch

In turn I slow my instincts   I know
to take in all the marvels as you give them me
So many pictures of 'The Dreams'

Love in the organ loft
for Marian

The cathedral lay feeling rather damp among its trees
and lawns, lichen covering its white stone walls
near the ground that is still wet from a rain shower.
It is April – of course. (Why should songs have all
the good lines? – like 'I love you', too.)

I'm beginning to wonder what I'm doing
and what is going on? All I know is that it's now
very late at night, or early in the morning . . .
You see, even this is disturbing and disordered.
Is someone weeping in the street outside?
It sounds like a man. It is 3.30 a.m.
But when I go to the window, I can see no one.
I might have asked him in to cry in the warm,
if he'd wanted. This isn't as stupid as it seems.
But everything on this (surface) level is so disjointed
that it can make even this possible act of kindness
appear to 'THEM' as 'foolishness' (if 'they' feel patronizing)
or 'absurdity' (if 'they' feel insecure that day).

At 5.00 a.m. I am still watching over my love
I love her more, so much more, than I've ever loved anyone,
even myself. In fact, this is a completely new
experience of *love*, like it is the first REAL time,
and love for real.

                        'My eyes hurt now, but birds begin
to sing outside anticipating the dawn – though I can find
no connection. Why should I? How absurd can I get
in this county town of the south-west province?

There appear to be no limits anywhere anymore.'
'His lips were sealed.' 'What is going on now?
You needn't doubt that I'll just wait –
"Faites vos jeux" – until I get to the bottom of this.'

The cathedral and its own lush green and garden,
and the comfortable and quietly rich church houses
with their private gardens that are set out
around the green – they are all peaceful and certain.
There is no question of escapism. (And it's about time
I woke up to this fact and appreciated the possible
sincerity of many such people and bodies.)

The birds masquerading as a 'dawn chorus'
have now become quite deafening with their twitterings
– I am sending for a shot-gun sales catalogue.

But what can this mean? – that I should
sit here all night watching over my love
and at the same time I fix
more than double my usual intake
to feel without compassion my brain wince
under chemical blows.

I mean what is happening? – NOW!   Do you see
what I mean? like does the cathedral nestle
in the sky's warm lap? *OR*   does the sky
respectfully arch over the cathedral's gothic
towers and roof, flying buttresses and pinnacles?
This parable can be used for most things – think of a river . . .

The belief that ignorance is usually cloaked
in pompous wordiness seems well proven
by everything put down so far. And, in fact,
anyone feeling the need to relieve his by now strong
resentment of me will be, when possible,
met in all humility. I accept my guilt

and am not surprised at these numerous 'accidents'
that seem to follow my progress through this city,
like falling slates and flower pots.

But please, when you all feel relieved,
will someone tell me how it is I am
so blessed at last with a real love
– and this like I've never seen possessed by anyone?
But also . . .   and yet . . .

And yet I know I need no explanations
and, least of all, justifications. The fact that the woman
I love with such continual and intense joy
and find what was before always transitory
an eternal and unshakeable happiness. All this
   is this is this is this . . .   I'm so happy;
and now as she turns in her sleep
her face's beauty fills me with a tenderness
and adoration that surprises even me, and fills my eyes with
   happy tears.

It's 6.00, and with the morning light
it seems my guard is over. No one comes
to relieve me – I couldn't stand rivals.
But why is the morbid masochism
of lines 46 to 47 still around? – Has it
no sense of decorum? All I want is to be able to
love as I'm loved and make my love happy.
Nobody here wants jack-boots,
or sleek vicious cars, or sleek vicious lovers,
or cocktail cabinets that play 'Jingle Bells'
everytime you open the doors – 'Oh boy!'.
All we want is ourselves – and that *is* really great.

But, please, if anyone has any answers
to the little problem of diet, do tell me.
I must go to bed now, but messages

can always be safely left here. Goodnight.
Good morning.
                         The cathedral is so pretty
here, especially in spring – so do visit.

Exeter
April 1967

The nine death ships

1

'This isn't the Black Forest!' he cried. But the sky was *so* blue.
'Do come in and put your revolver on the sideboard.' And so,
many days passed. It all became very neat and tidy. The house
was swept clean and all the revolvers put in a drawer suitably
labelled.
'I'm getting closer.'
'You sure are.'

2

The three men were very persistent, to the extent that they
even became boring. The servants were appropriately
informed. Only the dogs looked glum at the new situation.
'BANG!' – that changed it.
'My sweet, you see what I mean?'
The carriage continued ignoring the man who quietly read a
newspaper.

3

Manhattan is not at all confusing if one appreciates logic. I do,
for one.

4

The little house was so full of people that inevitably one of the
walls gave way – but, surprisingly, nobody was injured or
upset in the least.
'What a magnificent garden you have.'
We lolled the whole afternoon.

It was impossible to count the number of woodpeckers in the flock. But, unperturbed, they continued to wreck the country's entire telegraphic system.

The shot-gun blasted away.

5

'My eyes hurt from doing so much finely detailed clerical work in such a badly lit office.'

That was how the report began.

Death was so near, it became a shy joke among the inmates.

6

There was a small black book on the well scrubbed table in the lighthouse. You could hear the sea pounding the walls outside. Inside the book were stuck several photographs of gravestones in wintery graveyards. It was late winter. There were also some postcards which portrayed the deaths of various characters. One was an obvious choice – 'The Death of Chatterton' – painted by Henry Wallis. But the oval photo of Miller was not at all expected. The caption simply said 'MILLER / Northfield Bank Robber / Killed on front of Bank, Sept. 1876.' He lay naked and dead on the mortuary slab. The photo shows only his head, shoulders, chest and upper-arms. There were two obvious bullet holes – one low in his left shoulder, and the other high in the middle of his forehead. But it was only the first wound that had a stream of blood running from it.

The noise of the storm had by now grown quite deafening. It was impossible to hear what anyone said, no matter how loud they shouted. I was then further upset by the discovery that I was alone in the lighthouse. And it didn't look as though anyone would ever return. It was not even known if there had been anyone there to leave in the first place. It was all very confusing, and it seemed that I never would meet the owner of the small black book. For the while he certainly showed no intentions of returning for it.

I carried on whittling and putting ships in bottles.

Spring ploughing would be our next worry.

7

The houses were all yellow and the ladders green – such a conscious plan of life and its colours could only be described as 'revolting', and that was being too kind by far.
The lush red of blood, though, and all its varying moods and hues was a continual source of surprise and joy.
'Don't worry.'

8

'It was raining so hard and all the games had been played. There was nothing for it – we would just have to spend the afternoon watching the servants play leap frog. What a bore.'

Luckily he never finished his memoirs.

9

It seemed that the worst was over. The iron black fleet had finally steamed out of the bay. There was no communication. But at dawn the horizon was still empty. The sea was slate grey. If only this had been 'the worst' – but nobody can tell. The year was unsure – maybe it was 1900 or 1901.

The orchestra had to be slaughtered – they put everyone's nerves on edge. It was only through luck that Stravinsky escaped. That would be funnier if it was a joke. Insanity is always terrifying and illogical in its own logic.

As a distraction, let's not forget 'the amusing woodpeckers' or 'the surprising shot-gun' or 'the confusing yet simple street map of Manhattan'. They all serve some purpose – whatever that is.

The Sinking Colony

Linen

waking on the purple sheets whose softness
The streets heavy with summer   the night thick with green
   leaves
drifting into sleep we lay
The dazzle of morning   the hot pavements
fruit markets   'The Avenues'

'You and I are pretty as the morning'

on the beaches
machine-gunning the fleeing army
the fighters coming in low 'at zero'
the sun behind them   and bombs falling all round
'Jah Jah'   CLICK CLICK   'Jah Jah'

the cheap pages crumbling already after so little time
St Petersburg renamed the Soviet Printing House maybe

you leave the town   'the softness' like a banner
though where
In the countryside the trees bare and scrub bushes
scattered in useless fields
the darkness of a stand of larches
called 'the dark woods' on no map

touching you   like the
and soft as
like the scent of flowers and
like an approaching festival
whose promise is failed through carelessness

Death of a pirate king

1

A small train quietly follows the coastline.
The sky is so blue over the boat-yards, and the sun is a
blinding white
Meteorology.

At dusk the fishermen climb aboard the train and clutter the
carriages with their rods and baskets. At 'two o'clock' it's as
deserted as a shingle bar.
The green carriages. You're surprised. I can't explain *all* the
echoes. The lancers.

2

Ricochets make it dangerous for everyone in town, regardless
of their, or any, involvements. On the horizon clouds of dust
signal that the indians were tearing up the railroad again and
cutting telegraph wires AS USUAL. This lack of imagination
has something of the primitive in it. Alas. 'N'est-ce pas?'

3

Banditry.

4

That ridiculous gun-shot. Outside it's raining, maybe. It's like
the dream that is repeated so often that it comes true.

The window open, the curtains flapping, somehow suspended.
It is the 'softness' I'm talking about . . . Outside the countryside is seen in vague outline. It is 'an obsession with the
artificial'. Make way for hills and the noise of people milling
in the courtyard outside.
'Rolling.'

The words

Clouds scattered across the sky   all so far away
and then the space between   this strange 'distance'
What does 'normal' mean, after all?   you move
toward the window   lights marking the headland
and the night becomes a milestone   though
I   the fog rolls up the hill from the sea
in waves   the town   *desperate*?
Whichever way we look   though so much at hand
only held back by obsessions
but 'home' is so long ago   don't cry

the light's a very pale blue   then maybe   the next time
   too
a faint glimmer across the bay   neither moon
nor stars
and your letter making signs   concerning 'understanding'
and 'the magic tortoise'   what then?   or just tiredness

At each alternative   the colours in the sky
gradually changing   until you're lulled into believing
you've seen this before   but not quite
The wood-cut of a lone horseman
riding through a deathly countryside   raped

'You're very brave'   I clean the table-top
and you sat in that chair   two red poppies
in the garden below   at dawn
This apparent clumsiness is far from true

Cargo

As strange as the white cargo boat
heading east along the coast
two speed-boats named 'Dark Red' and 'Dark Blue' shooting
off
in glorified arcs of spray   like you
naked again   beyond the Green Mountains' snow
licked clean   puzzled
running out of petrol smells

'Will the hostages ever be freed?'
there's no echo from the mountains
nor a messenger to be seen running in the distance towards
us
There were many journeys . . .
But the dance-tune was not titled 'The Chains'
– 'How ridiculous!'

I reach forward and suddenly it's night again
and too dark for the jetty or the country walk
Such confinement is curious and absorbing
like an obscure scientific diagram   the combinations seem
limitless
yet it is the same base that's returned to   for years?

Now you have dressed
and tidied yourself
– all is ready for 'Departure'
and you manage skilfully
against such a background
and the sky this clean

Animal days

1

'The polo season would start early in April
so there was no time to be wasted.'

the night growing darker   the black plains
and below   the bright lights of the town

'knights on horses'? 'gentle ladies'? 'towers in the forest'?

it was as though your eyes filled with glass tears
crying some strange

there were peacocks on the high balconies
and a golden light   in fact 'a heavenly rod'
came down from the heart of a clear blue sky
you see

2

'You're right, even though you won't accept it.'

. . . with all the rifles brought back to safety
even the glimmer of polished metal

Buzzards, kestrels and hawks
circling high above the valley

the dust of the road   dazzling
with the white gates shut   do you understand
the garden so enclosed, and too green?

3

food is so very good

it is very black these days

the malevolence on the winter island

and what approaches in the darkness

beyond all knowledge   'the endurance'
surviving the fear

'but we're all so afraid'

and the children?

the indian chiefs
what are the wounds, anyway, and their cost?

In the morning everything is white
low clouds trail across the upper pastures
and the valley is thick with mist

'sometimes their canoes only hollowed-out tree trunks'

4

standing in the shadows or maybe in the distance
he   Like a long arcade or cloister
It was far from the grim scenes of the north
In his red tunic

The morning spent loading cord-wood onto a trailer

five young foxes in the bean-field waiting for the wood-
   pigeons

in the beech woods up on the ridge – the bark
still green and wet, the 'sticks' just felled.

It's reduced to a violent struggle
with heavy machinery, and boredom

the castle crumbling sedately   'damn fool!'
the gilding already flaking off

Cutting it up into 'blocks' on the saw-bench
The forest floor all torn up with bulldozer tracks
the soil a bright red   exposed below
the white shale backbone of the ridge

the sun sinking lower
the whole forest dripping moisture and green

the old railway station

5

holding a young rabbit in my hands
walking across the stubble in the late afternoon

soft fur   shocking like the heart-beat

the dark river   and angry knights milling
in the courtyard

setting it free in a hawthorn thicket
safe from the dogs

at night the land so bare   'rustles'

'They have no tradition of keeping their colonies neat.'

'I care for that woman' the song began

6

squandered in a matter called 'the heat of the moment'
not knowing what

'. . . at dusk the sound of church bells from the valley floor,
an owl flying low over a passing tractor.'

white with rain

The corrugated-iron roof of the mission discoloured
with rust   the deep green of the jungle
in the humid gorge

Like oppressors   striking fear into people
with threats of pillage and 'no quarter'

Inside the walls where
'No!'
too heavy   on evenings like this

in the courtyard
'the battlements'

The sinking colony

> 'This might almost make one suppose
> that he loved Bernard? . . . No; I
> think not. But a little vanity is quite as
> effectual in making us pose as a great
> deal of love.'
>
> Gide

1

At the time being a young geologist with the British Raj in India I was somewhat limited in the actions I could take, you see

The expeditions into the foothills and mountains to the north with our mules strung out behind us along the mountain track

At the base camp

Back at the bungalow my young wife was wearing her long white dress. The dark mahogany rock specimen cases glowed in the half light of our bedroom

Standing on the verandah in each others arms, the first monsoon rains kicking up dust in the compound, the servants rushing excitedly to the stables

Though it was considered rather eccentric, we would, when we had sufficient funds, hire local musicians to play for us in the evenings. They would sit on the verandah while we would sit inside in the darkness. The servants *would* chatter, *noisily*.

2

The heavy iron gates were swung open revealing beyond
a rich countryside at dusk

'COME IN'

tentatively on the dirt path   ahead a dark cloud of purple
and unnerved by the sounds   the footsteps
brushing stones

Beyond in the mountains or rather the foothills it was harvest
time

3 **The ache?**

There was a time of waiting while the rains lasted

It was cruel by nature of its very calculation, yet equally to
judge this as coldness is a mistake, rather it was a form of
preservation, a manufactured aim to allow time for some
possible movement to come about

This is clumsy, but like a mould made to hold the final
object and then be destroyed or forgotten once the real
purpose was achieved – though such neatness in explanation
is always suspect

There were complexities

4

To continue

The mansion was set in magnificent grounds
The trees were heavy with rain
and the fields of barley beaten down by summer storms

Haven't we been here before?
(sigh)   the impressive agricultural machinery
waiting for the dew to dry
You don't really need meters though to test moisture content

It seems so little is clear
The big house called 'The Mansion'
and the cold damp

What are we expecting, after all?
The pain goes through its cycle alternating
with the sunny days
but can you look it 'in the face'
and then continue skipping?

5 **Canadian days**

The inventory seemed endless. Let's start again –
    Moose
    Snow shoes
    Tins
    Sap
    Maple juice buckets and cauldron
    Axe
    Spare whale bones
    Sledge.
I can't work it out

  'I was out in the bush felling timber at the time. I had my
own team of horses, a good one. Things looked good.'
(We turn the page)
  'The maple tappers were passing through the district but no
one was expecting trouble.'

  It was suddenly colder than anyone could ever remember.
Cracking noises all through the night.

6

They stumbled out into the clearing
We just stood there
Then everything was thrown into confusion
– someone fired a shot
the horses bolted and the dogs tied themselves in knots

The rusted iron gate at last fell from its hinges
– someone *had* been tampering with the padlock

What could we do with all this?

Somehow even in the dreams we all needed one another
though there was little comfort in this

The Long Black Veil:
a notebook 1970–72

'things have ends (or scopes) and beginnings. To know what
    precedes   and what follows
    will assist yr / comprehension of process'

Ezra Pound – Canto 77

'In the Congo what joy could I take in gathering unknown
flowers with no one to whom I give them?'

André Gide – Journals, 31 March 1930

Preface

How to accept
this drift

the move   not mapped
nor clear other than in
its existence

a year passed
I think of you
it's early on a sunny morning in June
and think of your thinking of me
possible

How do we live with this?
yet live with this

What have we *left*
from all *this?*

      'Concepts promise protection
from experience.
          The spirit does
not dwell in concepts. Oh Jung.'
        (*Joanne Kyger* – DESECHEO NOTEBOOK)

two years passed 'Oh Jung'
the cycle not repeated
only the insistence

The story is that, when a child, Borges used to come to his father. His father would have a number of coins that he would place on his desk one by one, one on top of the other. To be brief – the stack of coins is an image of how our memory distorts and simplifies events the farther we move from them. The first coin is the actual event, the next coin is the event recreated in the mind, the memory, the next coin is a recreation of the first recreation, etc., etc., . . .

But what of the essence of this? 'Oh Jung's' insistences. The Sufi story of the famous River that tried to cross the desert, but only crossed the sands as water 'in the arms of the wind', nameless but

Book One

the soft dawn   it's light
I mean your body   and how I ache now
yes, tremble
                    the words?   how can they . . .

somehow the raven flying through endless skies
that ache too much   the unbearable distance
borne

Across the valley the sun catches the white silos
of these scattered farms
Up on the ridge

I mean following the creek . . .

As we lie in each other
dazed and hanging like birds on the wind

your body, yes   I'm talking about it
at last   I mean this *is* the discovery
Need I list the items?

On your way from the thorn tree to the house
you stop and half turn
to tell me . . .
that doesn't matter
but your look
and this picture I have
and at this distance

I have this now
I have what I have
                    in my hands

dawn – light – body – words – raven – skies – ache – distance
– valley – sun – silos – farms – ridge – creek – each other –
birds – wind

The Flight – BA 591

Book Two

Baseball in Central Park.

Anti-war parade on 5th Avenue.

The Egyptian rooms in the Metropolitan.

Reading Gide's 'Journals' in my room.

On the bus: the green Catskills. large black birds standing in the grass. wild blue iris in the swamps. two woodchucks. two rabbits. If other men's shoes fit, wear 'em.

We swim naked in the pool at night. The stars so bright. The hot night, the crickets and frogs singing. I hold you to me in a small room – the night air so heavy. Inside 'the dream' . . .

A farm dog barks somewhere across the valley.

The bright greens of the woods, the sun streaming down through the branches. The crashings of a chicken hawk suddenly startled and flying up through the branches to the safety of the sky again. The rain that increases and

thunder in the distance
the air heavy
and the valley white with mist

our bodies wet

As dawn breaks
we wake
and make love
again
the sky grey outside
and the birds singing

The sun comes up
You rise and make coffee
The woods so green

We go back to bed and

I can hear your footsteps
going about the house
doing things
while I sit by the window
of this upstairs room

the birds singing
in the heavy afternoon
the muffled sounds of a t.v.
downstairs

that I want you
this is why

I will call anything that goes on in my head 'a dream', whether
it be thoughts or imaginings, daydreams or sleep dreams. They
all give pictures of 'the possible', and that is exactly their value.

the two warships ploughed out to sea
waves flowed between them
as though dolphins lovingly touched each hull
in turn   No flecks of dust on the captain's
fine uniform   All the brass polished

Not the first   but one of many
such expeditions

Book Three

1:00 p.m., check into the hotel. It has two rooms and a bar. The town has two stores, three bars, a post office, church, gas station, fire station, and a small country library. People drive into town in their pick-up trucks, but it's not *that* 'country'.

Evening time out on the front porch step, smoking a cigar, watching the cars and people pass. Night bugs flying round the lights. Young men driving in pegs, putting up tents back of the fire station ready for the weekend 'Fire Department Chicken Fry'. The hot heavy night bringing the thunder and warm rain. Go to bed, the noise of passing trucks and the juke-box downstairs.

The fascination with *this* formality, *this* ritual.

Woken up early in the morning by the thunder, and rain beating on the tin roof of the porch. When I get up the air so soft and sweet. The square and hillsides a soft white with the fine mist. In the bar local farmers and workers from the nearby steel mills talking – '. . . a nigger wench, not a nigger woman . . .'. As I leave the sun breaks through on to the lush greenness of this valley.

Walk up the ridge west of the town – the minnows darting in the creek. The rock bed, and the currents there. The smell of young ferns as I walk up the hill through the beech woods.

Go up to the wild strawberry patch again, squat down and eat some. Continue up along the road, the pine woods by the crest of the ridge   'see for miles'

You walk through the door
No, now you stop your car in a small town square
I get up from the porch step and greet you
This is all 'country manners'

There's no steamer bringing you to me
up-river at the hill-station
No long white dress on the verandah

It is . . .
I hold you.   Isn't this enough?
The feel of your breasts
          beneath your loose white shirt

'It was used by the commentator of the Himyarite Ode, either
at first hand or through the medium of Hamdani's *Iklil*. We
may regard it, like the commentary itself, as a historical
romance in which most of the characters and some of the
events are real, adorned with fairy-tales, fictitious verses, and
such entertaining matter as a man of learning and storyteller
by trade might naturally be expected to introduce. Among the
few remaining Muhammadan authors who bestowed special
attention on the Pre-Islamic period of South Arabian history,
I shall mention here only Hamza of Isfahan, the eighth book
of whose Annals (finished in 961 A.D.) provides a useful
sketch, with brief chronological details, of the Tubba's or
Himyarite kings of Yemen.'
(R.A. Nicholson – A LITERARY HISTORY OF THE ARABS)

The small town set in a valley winding between ridges,
the lush green, the white mist at dawn,
the creek bed almost dry,
white scattered boulders and the willows.
The meadows so deep, and floating on their surface
the yellow and orange flowers.
The cool beech woods on late afternoons.
You melt into this landscape
and this only a description of my love for you

At the hill-station   all the bearers fled

The delighted naturalist was left unconcerned
carefully placing his specimens in the black metal box

'. . . and when he spoke about it to his friends they smiled and
said they found the comparison *odd*, but they immediately
dropped the subject and went on to talk about something else.
Hebdomeros concluded from this that perhaps they had not
really understood what he meant, and he reflected on the
difficulty of making oneself understood when one's thoughts
reached a certain height or depth. "It's strange," Hebdomeros
was thinking, "as for me, the very idea that something had
escaped my understanding would keep me awake at nights,
whereas people in general are not in the least perturbed when
they see or read or hear things they find completely obscure."'
(*Giorgio de Chirico – HEBDOMEROS*)

Book Four

We choose our condition

the sun shines
the warmth and softness of your flesh
'belly to belly' (like the song says)

The air so clear up on the ridge
this light
and then looking down to the valley

'our condition chooses us'
she says

In the morning we go for a drive, buy cakes and
milk, and picnic by the creek. The afternoon
spent in the meadow. In the evening we make love
in the room.

the sun glittering   through the glass
scattering rainbows on the walls and ceiling
the soft turf beneath the trees outside
your room where we lie naked
with our love

the country music plays
the words sung
'Palms of victory, crowns of glory,
   Palms of victory I shall wear.'

. . . felt so good this morning – as though I woke up beside
   you.

Book Five: Canadian Days

On the Northlands train from Toronto up to North Bay, Cochrane, and Kapuskasing. Then bus on to Hearst ('Moose Capital of the North'), and a jeep ride out to Jogues.
The night before the train full of drunks and bear hunters. Ridiculous. 'No guffing'.

And today early morning, the grey dawn. The 'towns' we stop at just a collection of huts scattered at random around the rail halt and a dirt road. And then the bush again. Heavy streams and rivers, and the forest cluttered with dead and fallen trees. The occasional windswept meadow, a grey weathered farmhouse deserted, fallen apart. Nothing. The bleak empty plain, marsh, lakes, the crowded conifer woods, a single silver birch in the middle of this.

The Northlands. The watery sunlight on dirt roads. The dull green country. Hardly any flowers to be seen.

At night the stars brighter than I'd ever seen them, and the curtains of light, the Aurora Borealis. This brightness dazzling, but it's with you that I want it.

It is the surface
your eyes
The foresters tramp in weary
Driven into a corner (so to speak)
to say this
I hold your head between my hands
your eyes

In the morning sitting on the front step, everything so calm and still. The warm sun, and a total quiet only broken by the bark of the ravens. The vast blue sky, and the forest stretching off on all sides. The long straight white dirt roads with a line of telegraph poles along side, and then the forest enclosing them on either side.

Book Six

The questions of complexity

On Gide's death Mr Forster said – 'I realized more clearly how much he had got out of life, and had managed to transmit through his writings. Not life's greatness – greatness is a nineteenth century perquisite, a Goethean job. But life's complexity, and the delight, the difficulty, the duty of registering that complexity and of conveying it.'

The distinctions

'Oh Jung' (1875–1961) on 'Marriage . . .' (1925)

The container *and* the contained
not *or*

one within the other
a continual shifting   and that both ways
– more a flow – from the simplicity to the complexity,
'unconscious' to conscious,
                                              and then back again?
and the move always with difficulty, and pain   a pleasure

not so much a repetition
but a moving around a point, a line
– like a backbone – and that too moving
(on)

yang and yin
light and dark

An island set among islands
and that no answer
But the need there –
somehow to have all one's hopes there,
to see and touch, to be wholly in one place.
Yet over the horizon   as real as any . . .
the ghosts
and them always moving

Before Completion   Wei Chi/64
But if the little fox, after nearly completing the crossing,
Gets his tail in the water,
There is nothing that would further.

                    in the half light . . .
A minotaur? a cat? tiger?   Her face
a metamorphosis   seen   at once   many times.
Our powers generating . . .
We touch, hold, and caress ourself

A bird flying high in the sky
above the clouds, and below them
an ocean, and a ship moving there.

'Such thoughts were very far from Julien's mind. His love was
still another name for ambition. It meant for him the joy of
possessing so beautiful a woman, when he himself was a poor,
unhappy creature whom men despised. His acts of adoration,
and his rapture at the sight of his mistress's charms, ended by

143

reassuring Madame de Rênal on the question of the difference in their ages. Had she possessed a little of that practical knowledge of the world which in the most civilized countries a woman of thirty has had at her disposal for a number of years already, she might have trembled for the duration of a love which apparently only existed on surprise and the transports of gratified self-esteem.'

(Stendhal – LE ROUGE ET LE NOIR)

Book Seven

My stomach   burns   Coming to you

How will . . . ?

The peaceful and flowering public gardens,
the smell of the ocean again
So much tied in such sites
of past pleasures

Stepping into the new   always   with you

A low haze beyond the harbour's mouth

I am full and happy   now   at your side

. . . we finally begin to fall asleep as dawn comes,
as a single whippoorwill starts to sing . . .

we wake, and make love. Outside a grey sea mist fills the
woods. Later, standing alone in these woods waiting for her,
not knowing how . . . this journey today so far from

The tricks are pulled

     blue skies flash across the screen

The falsity when anything becomes a symbol

You are lowered   very gently
into the waiting boat alongside

Much later   ashore on this island,
where tears rarely happen . . .

You are away there on other continents
So hard – 'It is hard to stand firm in the middle'
– waiting   for that lightness, that ease
of movement

The freighter was anchored in the middle of the bay with a
full head of steam up. As the launch approached

In the Museum of Fine Arts, Boston –

> *Mycerinus and his queen, Khamerernebty II*
> slate. fourth dynasty (2613–2494 B.C.)
> (The Pharaoh Mycerinus also known as Menkaure.)

In the Egyptian Museum, Cairo –

> *Mycerinus triad : Mycerinus, Hathor, and the*
> *personification of the 'Dog' nome.*
> slate. fourth dynasty.
> (The personification of the 'Dog' district
> (nome) is a woman.)

the tenderness. They stand facing us, she to his left, her right
arm around his waist, her left hand resting on his left upper
arm.

Horus, Hathor, Anubis.

Horus – the falcon headed god, the sun.

Hathor – the cow headed goddess, the sky.

Anubis – the jackal headed god, the guardian of the dead.

Horus, the rising sun, enters Hathor, the sky.
Obvious enough.

Doors flung open, a clear blue day outside, cactus, sage brush, and the yellow desert ochre, and the blue sky.   New Mexico.

Horus, son of Osiris, a falcon, whose two eyes are the sun and the moon, and whose breath is the cooling north wind.

Hathor, the cow, the sky goddess, stars on her belly, the sun between her horns, guardian of the Western Mountain, goddess of the copper mines of Sinai, of a woman's love and joy, of perfumes and spices, identified by the Greeks as Aphrodite. The mother who gives birth to Ra, the sun, at dawn. The destroyer on whose back Ra rides through the sky.

Anubis, the jackal, guardian of the desert cemeteries, master of embalmment, who oversees the weighing of each heart.

'a god is power personified . . . In Egypt . . .'

No godhead, no gospel, but 'a multiplicity of approaches', each in its own right, each immanent in nature.

Book Eight: England

So much either side of the immediate
though at its height – the love ecstasy
of the 'now' – it is only the immediate,
God's face.
(the Sufi poet, Ibn 'Arabi, writes of this)
God's face is the face of your lover.

I love you

the sky is full of wheeling gulls
Do I ask too much?
– the sea crashing white on the shingle –
that I'm torn apart each time you leave

the white buildings
the green sea and hills behind the town,
like some giant sandwich
and our love in the filling of it

You wheel above me

such whiteness

Christ, that I love you

how to deal with this?

I wait for you
not passively   but
I wait for you

My heart weeps

Who would ever have thought I'd write that?
'My heart weeps'?

'You must try, Psyche, to use up all your facility against an obstacle; face the granite, rouse yourself against it, and for a while despair. See your vain enthusiasms and your frustrated aims fall away. Perhaps you lack sufficient wisdom yet to prefer your will to your ease. You find that stone too hard, you dream of the softness of wax and the obedience of clay? Follow the path of your aroused thought and you will soon meet this infernal inscription: *There is nothing so beautiful as that which does not exist.*'

(*Paul Valery* – CONCERNING ADONIS)

Not a climbing, but a moving across the surface in a certain way, as though a soaking into the grain, what was there all the time, though never fully realized.

As though a monster haunts us – continually aroused at each 'wrong' word, each 'wrong' action, and roaring out from its darkness to terrorize us again. A giant and indestructible serpent filled with anger and venom, nightmare.

'Each single angel is terrifying' (*Rilke*)

Summer. The water meadows at dusk. The willows and long grass either side of the winding river, now only seen as a smooth black surface, the flow imperceptible. The buttercups indistinguishable in the growing darkness. Only the sound of your feet on the narrow gravel path. A cuckoo in a nearby spinney. The swallows out hunting. Across the fields the dim outline of the town – a clock strikes the hour, maybe in the church or the market-place.

Book Nine

Today, lying on the grass in the park
by your house
                   We were very close
Your husband, your children, you go
about your duties, you love
and care for them

Yes.

you there
me here

sometimes it's an ocean
spread between our bodies
sometimes only a matter of
yards across a carpeted room

you sit there
I sit here
there are people around us

the luxury
of setting eyes on you

You walk by my side through the park
what luxury
the

the cars the planes
the absurd mechanics
when all I want
is to walk up the hill to you

the silly girls clatter round
while you – the only woman I know,
the only woman I want –
are kept so securely from me
and at such a distance

a fierce wind tugs at the town
while I walk up the hill
and you on the other shore
while the sea bursts on this shore

there is a fine rain – I repeat myself –
it's night   there is a wind
To answer to . . . ?
when our world turns in us
dazzling
That hand offered us when the clouds part

'No, it's real,
 it's what I feel.'

(*by 'The Soft Machine'*)

The pride. Being with you, knowing very simply where I'm
going, where I stand, of being able to put aside all the half-
things and live with one sure knowledge of what matters,
what is.

'. . . an ease in the air around us that we can spread into . . .
and ideas are like stars instead of gravity – we're not held by
them by their necessities.'

(*your letter*)

151

Book Ten

The rain falling
you could be driving a car now
somewhere

You drive the car and my hand rests on your shoulder
the radio is playing
the rain is beating on the car roof
and the road is a brilliant black

the honour of you
'I am honoured' someone says

that I should cry now

we all know what this means
and there's no need for any rich details

when John said 'from egotistical to egocentric'
he was right about the process
there's no cause for shame

and the 'honour'?

the word grows emptier the farther it moves
from the flesh
while *my* honour lives in your flesh

'You're your own train, you got your own track, and you can
    go anywhere.'

(Fielding Dawson quoting Charles Olson in
    THE BLACK MOUNTAIN BOOK)

But you the ground,
earth I want,
the place

the luxury of it
to hold my reality in my arms

the touch
of it
you
the feel of you
so much now

Book Eleven

Is it the Rilkean dream or 'home' we come to?
At dusk the skyline obscure.
Yes and No.

Many pictures – the surface apparently the same.
A series of events, but the marks they leave varying. Things
happen, have qualities.

And ahead?
The mountains, the wind, the sea   are there
we move through them, across their surfaces

like a moving hunter

On a 'threshold'?   in the open
dazzled by the sunlight, and 'nervous',

but moving – and that with care.
No end.

But the quality

The dreams do happen –
and there is no 'home' we come to
– but on this earth, and open to its powers

A recognition of the ghosts that guide us. The dead watching
over us, surrounding us with a tenderness – as though they
were gravity – they hold us, their arms around us, however
we move.

And Anubis guiding the dead through their journey.

Before the tribunal of Osiris, Anubis, the jackal-headed god, watches over the weighing of the dead man's heart – the heart in one scale, and in the other an ostrich feather, symbol of Ma'at, the goddess of truth. And if the heart is truthful the dead man is led up to Osiris by Anubis and becomes Osiris, god of the dead, of the under world – that is, of the earth beneath our feet.

Book Twelve: California Journal

the eucalyptus groves on the mountain sides the road cuts through – no – follows the contour obediently. The coast . . .

the heat and wetness of us

later alone on the beach . . . the sandpipers rush about, following each wave out, picking the sand. The gulls

. . . through the barrier. 'That isn't pain, it's something else.'

driving through the mountains. San Anselmo. San Rafael. the redwoods. The ease of walking in the hot sun in California down a dirt path laughing, ordering milk-shakes, and watching the traffic pass. Of being totally in one place. The dry mountains around us. Nowhere else

At night the smell of orange blossom at the post-office

In the bar I talked with this man passing through town about Union matters.

'. . . For Beauty's nothing
but the beginning of Terror we're still just able to bear,
and we adore it so because it serenely
disdains to destroy us. Each single angel is terrifying.

              Ein jeder Engel ist schrecklich.'
              (*Rilke – DUINO ELEGIES 1*)

walk the length of the beach as far as the rocks watching the small and large sandpipers. Orange butterflies glide above the parking lot.

when we're together the time always so short. The minutes counted and noted down. And around these times the long hours of waiting.

that hot surface where our bodies meet, press together – 'a melting spot'.

she tells me of

                        the tearing

                                        leaving

            the only woman

We drive up into the mountains behind the beach. Muir Woods. Mount Tamalpais. The air so clear and sweet. On the short turf . . .   her laughing. She looks so beautiful.

In the evening in the room . . .

Making love, the final blocks clear. My body taken into her body completely, and then her body into my body.

In that place the ease there

more beautiful than ever, her black hair so thick and rich

She anoints my wrists

the anointment a ritual like the sweetening of the body before burial, before our parting. My not realizing the completeness of this until now.

In the distance the mountains — the dream echoed again and again in many parts, in many places. An antelope (not understanding this animal) lies down exhausted yet calm. Some form of quietness.

The ritual of – repeated again – No. We make love – to each other – in turn. The body glowing, dizzy . . . walking through clouds. The faces transformed again.

She accepts the objects – the stone, the orange blossom.
She gives the objects – the whittled twig, the dried seedpod.

She puts the bead bracelet around my wrist

lie naked upon the bed.

Qasida Island

Qasida

it's *that*
the quiet room
the window open, trees outside
'blowing' in the wind.
the colour is called green.
the sky.
the colour is called blue.
(sigh)   the crickets singing

windows open. You move . . .
No, not so much a moving
but the artificiality of containment
in one skin. 'No man an island' (ha-ha Buddha)
. . . lonesome, huh?

THE music, THE pictures
(go walkabout)
Small wavy lines on the horizon

somewhere over the distant horizon
the distant city (I hadn't thought of this,
but pull it in) and you

the children are sleeping
and you're probably sitting in the big chair
reading or sewing something
It's quarter past nine
I find you beautiful

*   *   *

the words come slowly. No . . .
your tongue   the lips moving
the words reach out –
crude symbols – the hieroglyphs
sounds, *not* pictures

the touching beyond this –
I touch you

in the water
as though I'm in you

that joy
and skipping in the street
the children hanging on our arms

      *   *   *

You know . . . – the signals (on the horizon?)
'blocked off'   the ships at night
keep moving

these clear areas beyond the clutter
that clearing

on summer nights as we lie together . . .

there are green trees in the street
yes, there is the whole existence of
our bodies lying naked together
the two skins touching
the coolness of your breasts
the touch

The setting . . .
it doesn't really matter
We know
So much goes on around us

on the quay they're playing music
we'll eat and dance there,
when the wind gets cold
we'll put our sweaters on
it's that simple, really . . .

                    *   *   *

. . . the dry fields
Up on the mountain sides
white doves (of course) glide
on the air-currents   hang there

someone said tumble
'the sound of words as they tumble
from men's mouths' (or something like that)

there are these areas,
not to be filled, but . . .

it's a bare canvas, but not empty –
all there under the surface

This is not about writing,
but the whole process
You step off the porch into the dry field
You're there
You see, you're *there*
Now, take it from there . . .

One, two, three

An emperor gives a gift, stylishly,
and a Mughal miniature records it
(colour and gold on paper, height $7^3/_{16}$ inches)

we're dazzled – all this art
and surprises   'Keeping the doors open'
Right?

Yes, I suppose, fascinated by the delicacy
of the piano part in the first movement
of Beethoven's 'Ghost' Trio
('he sighed . . .'   But real enough,
aesthetic coat-trailing aside.
The delight beyond the technicalities
– not pursuing, but there
to be recognized

We can see this

And all those private separations?

When 'we' moves from the general
to the particular?

To talk of *you* now . . . ?
amongst all this 'delight'
– moving into that other level –
the poverty of this, one without the other,
the delight more a refuge than any whole thing
when you're away

Up in the hills the court is assembled,
the gifts exchanged
From the balcony I see you cross a courtyard,
could almost touch you –
but the distance.
                              Be well.
the moonlight on your face
as you sleep now

                    *   *   *

hold me

outside the rain falling in the street
I hold you   your flesh so soft

to begin to say – 'I love you . . .'?

the heat of your belly

away   the hills
(Fuck 'the hills')

my mouth on your throat
my body smells of your body

                    *   *   *

There are many fields
and the fortresses are so far apart.
The troops stand in line on the parade ground
while the sun beats down on them
and their bored officers.

it's another day

meanwhile . . .

                    there are many settings

A group of men can sit stiffly
for a regimental photo of the survivors of the disaster,
and then try to look neat and alert.

And their children . . . ?
living in a calm beyond this knowledge?
It is not so much a question of guilt
on either side, but maybe some form of recognition
which rarely happens.

And the years pass until one generation dies
and their knowledge with them
leaving behind only feelings of confused longing
that quietly spread beyond any conscious resentment.

Now put it together.

New Year

for Shifrah Fram

a dark forest somewhere
with a chain of lakes
scattered between the mountains

no one for miles (literally)
except you   a white movement
among the trees   a 'blur'

but more precise than that

maybe a long way off a railway
but I think not
nor a moored seaplane on
one of the lakes

even the possibility of dirt roads
now seems remote

it is all very still
(like) some form of memory
the outline of your breast
seen clothed
in a crowded room

there is the sound of the wind
in the tree tops above you
and your feet on the pine needles below

fading to
the white area in which the 'blur' is lost

the journeys   moving
                    '. . . trying,
to get it right'

that past *now* present
and then . . .
                    we move

not circling but an
unknown progress

looking down the slope
through the trees to the lake
at times losing all sense of direction

now you enter a crowded store
in a large city

it is somehow impassive

'in control'   'our condition'

Five postcards to Alban Berg

1

waves break over the headland
the pain of closeness /'to a lover'
The mountains
walk in the mountains
The lightness of touch
clear air

2

the blue sky
(pan to) spring ploughing
and cattle grazing on the (green) slopes
the wild flowers abundant and   many coloured
Can you see now?   can I . . . ?
Many miles away . . .   Here

3

The dark night /'close to your lover'
the rain and wind outside

4

in the evenings as the sun sets
red skies and the swimming

the insult of an image
when it's only what's here before you

5

the skies clear   (blue)
midday   the moon still there
sheep deep in the flowers   daisies and poppies
Off beyond the distance 'you'
Minutes in the day when (maybe) the pictures cross
and focus
The island   firm
the mountains up into the sky   'beyond'

'Inside the harm is a clearing . . .'

There were clouds   the sky was heavy
the rivers were heavy with flood
The line of hills the mud green usual
after the thaw
Through the middle the glint of steel rails
In the valley is a small market town
almost a village

*   *   *

In the morning her white body
(it being north european) and the black hairs
Your desire is revived

There comes this desire
to be clean
This involves distance
There comes this decision
of the necessity
in moving
at the right time
in the right way

*   *   *

There are many steamers moored in the busy estuary
'Come here'   we lean over the rail
The town is a whole scatter of colours
Our clothes are immaculate and white

The kaleidoscope of the tropics yet the simplicity
As I bend to kiss you my lips brush your hair
Somewhere in the clearing

                    *   *   *

The clutter   Above the ridge
the colours heavy   washed through
and he said then
'every man to his junk-shop'
not moving but fixed
in those same games of 'identity'
Somehow a tight blue blanket
wraps us up
in the silly dreams
Your body

it's never like you dream it
turning this side and that

                    *   *   *

on the edge of town   the scattered houses
the Mill House roaring
people are walking through the water-meadows
it's a mild evening
we're taken in by the very aura
the famous cathedral
and the orchards on the hillsides
this softness could be in any season

They're like running figures
seen as white flashes in the green distance
towards the rails

* * *

'Soon we'll be there   a few more days
you'll like it
the bungalow   the cool verandahs
and our walks in the evening
Naturally my work takes up most of the day
but it's only right that way'

We walk round the deck
the other passengers smile at us kindly
like accomplices in the dream
we all know

As we get under way
a cool breeze comes up river
and ruffles your hair

North

Snow on the furrows
and on the hilltop the black castle and cathedral
and the close city like an island
ringed by icy rivers
The days briefer, even darker

It is the small and isolated fortress
that lies to the north
where you are left
your nakedness on some white winter day

The snow cover
the gardens of ancient houses thick with it
and then the stars

you know
we shiver at the contortions
but have to perform
the desperate dreams
that we so carefully build
in the long weeks of loneliness

Too cold to even touch the flesh
yet driven on in the heat of the obsession
dazed almost when raising the head
and seeing beyond the window

Split down the middle – what's happening?
The unreality at the wrestling match
and then so much neater to avoid any analysis
with the picture books all ready and the warm fire
The clean white schooner's fascinating voyage

Night ferry

'The hotels in the narrow side streets . . .'
appears automatic
and all part of 'the process' whatever that may be

and on the edges of town the sea
and some say the marshes
out of that deep tank of enthusiasm
we all admire so much

being cut in two
kissing round the borders of the hairs
and other reclining positions
back into the personal obscurity
of the obsession
Much grander sounding than when it
comes to crouching naked on all fours
'WOOF'
the animals range away happy as ever

It is the tortuous path threading between
the buildings

'WOOF' (again)

All leading to you and hunger
'I am obsessed with'

But

The travellers leave their bags at the station
and between trains visit the town briefly
It seemed worthless by virtue of its very shallowness
but how to reconcile their journey's necessities
with something nearing any real appreciation?
Can we say 'service'?

Country diary continued

'Ah, Hilda, my dear, you're so pretty.' (in a German accent)

and the shooting?

I used to shoot a bit in Africa, get a duck or so for supper. But there seemed to be such a lot of killing going on. I felt I could not add to it. I gave up shooting then, except for a little target practice. Lost the taste for it somehow.

'his patrol was ambushed by Zulus'

Today

I tidy the room
it all becomes a notebook or an excuse

> 'A bay seen through the window – it's a
> summer morning – the romantic coaster ploughs on
> leaving a smoky trail behind.
> At sea : 16 bells.'

From the window: cluttered back-yards

It's now down to a matter of lists
that act as buttresses, even defences.
No? the same tired and selfish stories?

Out there . . .

There seems to be great activity
and everyone has been invited to collaborate
It's all very curious and useless
I mean 'what body winds round what body?'
a poor excuse for 'intellectual search'
or 'a full and active life' –
though at times being 'in love' is a life in itself

The floor is swept and all the ledges meticulously dusted
the room is then well aired by opening the window wide
I'm left standing in the middle of the room
holding a wet cloth

There are too many accounts of cruelties
but the other side always sounds slightly false
or is an expression of nostalgia
But what can ache more than repetition?

Cut into slices?
Stuck in 'the vertical' – is that too obscure?

Boston to Brighton

Boston Spring

Song of praise?
the strong wind cutting across the river
blowing grit in the eyes of the pedestrians crossing the bridge
after visiting an exhibition of Indian miniatures
from the little valley kingdom of Kangra in the Punjab Hills
(N.W. India) painted in the late 18th century
or early 19th century?   I think not.

*   *   *

1) Take a bath.
2) Drink some chocolate.
3) Go to bed.

What else?

*   *   *

There are so many evasions
and the cunning fox knows all the
bolt holes and impenetrable thickets
in this particular patch of woodland.
Emergency Instructions by heart,
by rote, THAT IS
'rote, n. Mere habituation, knowledge got
by repetition, unintelligent memory.'

Brighton ● October

a cloud passes by
the stuffed animals in the museum
    continue to stare straight ahead

at sea three freighters wait on the tide
    to enter the small port

load of timber
cargo of coal

a man walks along the edge of a park
beneath the trees that have just begun
to shed their leaves

I am thinking of the forms of peace,
or, rather, pure pleasure

CHÊN

one of those

     rare

          moments

     when

thoughts of death
strike

The desire to hang on

     to what

        I have

to not   lose
sight

     of

       what's held dear

the line of hills

     that edge

(the) coast

     * * *

sometimes there is

the need

    to explain

make that mark

      clear

the clarity

    what believed

or rather hoped for

*   *   *

                    to be afraid   of

no action clear

    but

              sets of blocks

the hard rain at night

but with mornings

                          (so) clear

blue sky and sun

like spring   the winter

to move carefully

                    here

    but how

when so crowded

              by those fears

          *   *   *

'When a man has learned within his
heart what fear and trembling mean,
he is safeguarded against any terror
produced by outside influences.'

'Six in the fifth place means:

Shock goes hither and thither.

Danger.

However, nothing at all is lost.

Yet there are things to be done.'

      *   *   *

fear, v.i. & t. : to be afraid of,
hesitate to do, shrink from doing;
revere.

      *   *   *

'a long road'

        she said

'it's a long road'

fear of loss

the loss spreads   (as much)

through the future

       as in the past

Hauntings

    in the face of which

       we

survive somehow

'a long road'

Old Bosham Bird Watch
for Jud

1

out of nothing comes . . .

nothing comes out of nothing

cut   /   switch to

a small room, in a building of small rooms. 'Enclosed thus.'
Outside there are bare trees groaning and twisting in the wind.
A cold long road with houses either side that finally leads
down hill to a railway station. The Exit.

2

Out on the estuary four people in a small dinghy at high tide.
Canada geese and oyster catchers around. The pale winter
sunlight and cold clear air. Onshore the village church con-
tains the tomb of Canute's daughter, the black Sussex raven
emblazoned on the stone. Small rooms.

3

Sat round a fire. The black Danish raven rampant.
In the dream.
Enclosed, I reach out. She moves in her ways that the facts of
closeness, familiarity, obscure. Our not quite knowing one
another in that sense of clear distance, that sense that comes
with distance, like old photos making everything so set, clear,
and easily understood – so we think.
Face to face the changes flicking by second by second. Not the
face fixed that yes I know her. Not the easy sum of qualities

4

How long since you've known who you are? How long? Why
who you? Don't know. Long time. Only have old photos, old
images, old ikons peeling. That man who lived at X, did Y,
travelled to Z, and back, 'The Lone Gent'?
Why, who was that masked man? Why, don't you know?
NO !

5

In the closeness that comes with shared actions. From keeping
a room clean, keeping clothes clean, cooking a meal to be
eaten by the both of us. In that closeness, maybe on the edge
of losing something gaining something. Questions of clarity
and recognitions.

6

We swing hard a-port then let the current take us, the ebb
tide pulling us out towards the Channel. The birds about, the
colours of the sky, the waters, all the different plants growing
beside the estuary, and the heavy brown ploughed fields
behind these banks. Here, more than anywhere else, every
thing, all becomes beautiful and exciting – and the fact of
being alive at such moments, being filled with this immense
beauty, right, Rilke, 'ecstasy', makes the fact of living immeas-
urably precious.

7

Enclosed by cold in the winter. The clear sharp days walking
down hill looking out to sea, the wind up, the waves crashing
on the shingle beaches. And the days of rain and harsh grey
skies, coming home from work in the dark through the car
lights and shop lights. The exit always there. I can't say I
'know' you. But neither can I say what 'knowing' is. We are
here, and somehow it works, our being together.

8

The sky, the gulls wheeling and squawking above, the flint walls of these South Saxon churches, the yew trees branching up into that winter sky. I know these. But not what you're thinking, what anyone is thinking. I can never know that, only work with that — as it comes. Open arms open air come clear.

9

The dinghy is brought ashore. The people drag it up the bank and carry it to the cottage where they stow it neatly. Everything 'ship shape'. Out to sea the coasters head for Shoreham and Newhaven. Along the coast small blue trains rattle along through Chichester, Littlehampton, Worthing, and on to Brighton.
The fire is stoked up in the small room. The people in the cottage all eat dinner together, are happy in one another's company.
That I love you, we know this, parting the branches and ferns as we push on through the wood.

Machines

1

In the darkness you could hear hooting noises, ahead? some-where 'out there'. As though ships were passing in the nearby estuary. Or maybe a distant freight-yard. In such blackness the strings of yellow lights 'illuminating the scene' could only be imagined. The stacks of timber and oil drums, the quiet of the night.

Across the field maybe the dark outline of a wood? That's another possibility.

Enclosed in such a state. The dark pressing in, felt brushing one's face and hands, 'the soft fur of nights'.

2

In the darkness of the cottage, midday, and the large stone fireplace filled with wood ash. Up behind the cottage the beech woods, below, the steep green slopes down to the valley. The trees and valley a soft grey white with the mist and drizzle of early autumn. In the darkness of the cottage . . .

'breaking down at the continual brutality of it all, and my failure, once again. The tears flow down my face. I bury my head in the arms of the woman I've also failed.'
A mile and a quarter walk away a black farm raincoat lies neatly folded up beside a tall hedge with a sharpening stone and bill hook on top of it.

IMAGINE an elegant octagonal room with a high ceiling. The room is about 30 foot across and has french windows along the four sides of the room that face south. These windows look out over extensive lawns that finally end in a shrubbery and woods. It is a summer afternoon with clear blue skies as far as you can see. The time is about 2.30 p.m.

The room itself feels pleasantly warm and airy. The walls are painted white and in their decoration and the matching mouldings on the ceiling show the house to be built in the 18th century in the Georgian neo-classical style. The floor is parquet and polished to a fine and rich glow. The only furnishings in the room, which is otherwise bare, are a Persian rug and a small table. The rug lies on the north side of the room and measures 10 foot by 6 foot. Its colours are generally lighter than usual and the abstract design less elaborate. The small oval table stands in the middle of the room.

On this table stands a machine of some sort, or maybe it could better be called a mechanism or instrument. The instrument is about 3 foot high and at its mahogany base measures one foot by one foot. The overall impression is that of a neat and complex arrangement of brass joints and mechanical parts, and shiny steel rods, all in motion that is both smooth and dignified. Atop the mechanism a steel foliot rod rotates slowly, the two brass balls at either end glinting as they turn. This escapement regulating, as they say, the transfer of energy from the spring to the various gears. The whole machine is a combination of many such correct regulations. Stepping back from it and closing your eyes you hear well oiled clicking noises against a background of the distant noises from the gardens outside. A blackbird singing and the sound of a small group of people approaching the house.

1a

'It's cold enough, tonight?'
'Oh yes, it is that.'

2a

'How are you? OK?'
'Yes, fine. Right.'

3a

'Well, of course facts must be true, but when it comes to it that's kind of irrelevant. I mean the story is where the work is done.'

4a

Nikolaus Pevsner: 'The English portrait conceals more than it reveals, and what it reveals it reveals with studied understatement.'

5a

'Yes, well, that may be so, but I still find it difficult to accept.'

6a

. . . a startled blackbird winged up through the beech woods, finally disappearing into the delicately leafed tops, its cries echoing on long after
This isn't nature poetry.

Wish you were here: six postcards

for Antony Lopez

Preface

Great clouds of sadness and poverty cross the sky
shadowing the land below and the people's minds
The wind strong and bending the young trees

At the coast there is, yes, a brightness
the crashing of waves on the pebble beaches
the cliffs a dazzling white wall either side of the haven

The autumn with those weeks of white mist mornings
and afternoons where the light itself takes on a golden haze
All of this surrounding and filling us – the giant clouds and
  the bright sea

The Walk, Abertillery Park

    to walk the paths where birds sing,
to at night see through the tree tops the whole scatter of stars

the humans and animals walk out in the darkness
night hunters while the birds sleep the planet turns

I can only talk of, at such times,
the wonder and the loneliness of this

Population figures fade in the apparently endless shelves of
statistical registers. Mr Jamesson turned to close the small low
gate behind him then walked at a brisk pace down the road,
fearful as ever of being late for work. His telescope and bird
books lay waiting in the front-room for the weekend.

Tryst Road, Stenhousemuir

proud of watch and chain
proud of stone solid houses
proud of new coat and shoes
proud of being photographed in this cold bleak treeless street

a lump of tenderness sticks in our throat
while 'SENTIMENTALITY' flashes on the screen
but proud, all the same, of the continual struggle
of people
to survive and make despite

'I have always felt that I was living on the high seas, threatened, at the heart of a royal happiness,' wrote Camus. And
Stevenson too on his first long sea voyage spoke of being filled
with a total happiness he'd not known before, his health and
spirits being completely revived by the experience.

And wasn't it at a cottage in Stenhousemuir he started to
write 'Treasure Island'? Maybe I confuse the names and the
town was really called Braemar. But whichever – a bleak
place.

Rue de la Pierre, Messines

Camus wrote of Gide:
'I had never met him before, and yet it was as if we had always known each other. Not that Gide ever received me very intimately. He had a horror, as I already knew, of that noisy promiscuity which takes the place of friendship in our world. But the smile with which he greeted me was simple and joyful and, when he was with me, I never saw him on his guard.'*

and in Messines the grim peasantry stand around in the cold bright sunlight of this particular winter's day. The clear blue sky goes unremarked by the minor officials who are busy with their mean business. Hard and mean as a peasant's heart, someone might say, and these, their sons, continue the tradition even though decked out in uniforms and the occasional modest decoration.

In the picture rue de la Pierre goes straight ahead then disappears to the right. And out in the icy countryside an avenue of standing stones goes *its* own way straight across a stretch of bleak moorland radiating some other kind of strength and that wonder shut out elsewhere.

yet the coldness that grips one's whole body

someone unseen opens the double doors within the apartment and the stranger steps through smiling. We are filled with his warmth, his face like the sun.

* Albert Camus, *Encounters with André Gide*

Maison Desgardin, Route De Gameches, Tours-en-Vimeu (Somme)

To make one song of praise,
even on a flat muddy plain,
in weary farmlands and hard factory towns
To praise those gentle and careful acts
people *do*

The family with a large dog that live in a small new house
on the edge of town
Each with their own distinction
The knowledges and unknown skills of *other* people
never to be taken for granted, ignored.
Each one

Rays of sun breaking through the slate grey clouds
and spot-lighting a gentle ridge of hills,
a clump of trees, two or three small fields
And in the air the bird song,
the clear music

Blick Auf Grimselgebiet

I think of you
I think of the walk down through the pine woods to the village
I think of the questions of affection,
of those that were dear to me and
those that are dear to me

And at this point the quiet and loneliness of
a deserted hotel balcony overlooking an Alpine valley . . .

Yes, here in the mountains far from any sea,
snow on the peaks, the cool air of evening
scented with resin from the pines, early spring

A lengthy description merely buys time, can go on
filling many pages – the excuses
for failure and the inability to clear air in the midst of clear
air,
rather sinking back into the luxury of refined loneliness,
of cultured thoughts and a general fascination with
the 'finer points'

Opening the book that he had earlier carefully placed on the
white table cloth, he continued to read a collection of short
stories by Bruno Schulz. The beginning of one story particu-
larly struck him with its appropriateness to his present mood.
It began: ' "The Demiurge", said my father, 'has had no
monopoly of creation, for creation is the privilege of all spirits.
Matter has been given infinite fertility, inexhaustible vitality,
and, at the same time, a seductive power of temptation which
invites us to create as well.' "

The air was so sweet. The white linen of the table cloth such a pleasure to his eyes and his touch. It seemed anything was possible when he had such a sure sense of where he was and what he was doing at this very moment. Everything would follow naturally from this. The word 'flow' is maybe more accurate than 'follow'. Everything would flow from this without the hindrance of nervous plans or plodding schemes. It would just flow, glide through the air like some amazingly beautiful and powerful bird of prey, like the buzzards that circled this valley.

Contrejour sur La Plage, Saint-Enogat

Two boys splash along the beach

the streaked sky of late afternoon
the grand mansion silhouetted on the headland

as though the sun stranger lay in wait
ready to burst forth   but not today

let it rest
                hugged in the arms of the sea
naked
in bird song sea sway

Entering a bookshop in the capital I buy a copy of de Montherlant's 'Textes sous une occupation, 1940–1944'. I obviously see this choice, because of my great affection for it, as somehow more than apt for my present situation. As though I continually feel that I too live besieged and threatened by 'dark and brutal forces', and yet strive in spite of this to be open and fresh to all the wonders that do finally triumph over the invaders.

This would be as good a place as any for me to start writing my biography, for anyone to start writing *their* biography.

Sussex Downs

'I'm just in love with all these three,
The Weald an' the Marsh an' the Down countrie'

Rudyard Kipling

To fall in love with the countryside
and stay in that love
writing love poems

in one's head, one's eyes, one's fingers,
one's body   walking
through the hot July wheatfields
heady with the scent of camomile.

Poems beyond any words
of explanation
                and only left with the notebooks
                filled with lists and impressions:

'Delicate harebells trembling
above the white stars of the wild thyme
as I climb the ramparts of Cissbury Ring.'

'An electric-blue dragonfly
skims the dewpond near Chanctonbury Ring
where the beeches rustle in the sou'-west wind
and the Isle of Wight appears
like a huge misty whale on the horizon.'

As though all my life I've been approaching
this,
earlier carelessness behind me now,
being of that age
settled
      and eager to see what lives outside me:
the Downs that 'swell and heave their broad backs
into the sky'.

There are no ghosts here
but as though we lived forever,
all of history and ourselves alive in this one moment
in one place with no wish to be elsewhere.

from Notes of a Post Office clerk
for Harry Guest

'*For the heart of another is a dark forest . . .*'
Ford Madox Ford – ANCIENT LIGHTS, 1911

the faces blur, yes
but the actions carry through

Moving or not moving
the angle or degree matter little

except the realization
of the powers
we all wield

are responsible

      for what   we do

the act   politic

Storms blowing from the sou' west.
In the square the trees bend,
and make noise.
Spring tides highest for 300 years

Believe me

       *   *   *

Hollingbury

Above the earth fort

    a skylark   singing

        twittering

The stillness as

    the mists roll in

        from the sea

so clear

        the air

here

    the sun

        catching

the line of hills

    in the distance

    *   *   *

For three years
my lady and me
have lived in one room

I'm sick of living in one room
I'm sick of being poor
I'm sick of the rich taking from the poor
(and them pretending to not even know it!)

I'm sick of the rich.

*   *   *

sun in the skies

you're laughing   crying

it's all there

the pain   and the quiet pleasure

trains in the night going to
set destinations
but the events still unknown

I move, but not so much a matter
of invention, but what happens

*   *   *

the sea is grey green

flat

with heavy clouds low on the horizon
                              'low in the sky'

   the piers are set in the sea
the cliffs an off-white

               *   *   *

old men move

      walk by

      stand

      speak words

which we come

          to respect

that there is the trying

which we so love

that the words come
– through all the veils of *that*
date or *that* class
but which come – through

to show, make the marks
that show

a man cared and thought

and that his cares and thoughts

touch us

now

and push

us further in the trying

All the Wrong Notes

Text for an engraving

'In the wild end of a moorland parish, far out of the sight of any house, there stands a cairn among the heather, and a little by east of it, in the going down of the braeside, a monument with some verse half defaced. It was here that Claverhouse shot with his own hand the Praying Weaver of Balweary, and the chisel of Old Mortality had clinked on that lonely gravestone.'*

For on 8th July 1853 Commodore Perry sailed into the Bay of Yedo with his squadron of 4 US Navy ships, and established a base at Loo-Choo (Okinawa). And so one form of ritualised barbarism replaces another, I guess. The Japanese woodcuts portraying those four tall black ships have a beauty in their colouring that is a far cry from the probable ugliness of the incident.

Though these facts were so remote from her, she could certainly imagine 17th century Scotland or the establishment of western capitalism in Japan as she sat that afternoon in the top room. All around her were stacks of slightly worn and dusty furniture, piles of books, and large trunks filled with mementoes and 'things that will come in useful some day'. Outside the countryside and gardens were sodden. The rain soaked long grass bending over the swollen streams. Wet gusts of wind shaking the trees. In a late autumn such as this she could only sit, as though frozen, for afternoons that never seemed to know any progress. She imagined what it must have been like for Robert Louis Stevenson in the South Seas. How would his afternoon have gone at the Vailima estate on Samoa?

* R.L. Stevenson – Introductory to *Weir of Hermiston*

'. . . until about 2 when I turn in to work again till 4; fool from 4 to half past, tired out and waiting for the bath hour; 4.30 bath; 4.40, eat two heavenly mangoes on the verandah, and see the boys arrive with the pack-horses,' he said.

To be read very slowly
for Harry Guest

At two bells on the middle watch – unable to forget the cry of
wounded creatures deep in the wood. The bridge in near
darkness except for the yellow light glowing from the compass,
the instruments.

Haunted by a strange dream of a wild and thick wooded
country, a forested lowland with high bare ridges looking
down on all this, walling it in. The possibility of ruined
buildings made of stone lying somewhere within this forest,
in fact such sites scattered like dying stars throughout the
forest-land.

To wake from such dreams, sweating, and in a tangle of
bedclothes. To wrench open the port-hole and fill your lungs
with that clear sanity of sea air. To see the ocean again
sparkling with moonlight, reassuring us, always there.

But when struck with that dark hard reality of death how the
fear fills us again and again, whether awake or dreaming.
Both at the loss of all we love and hold dear, the gardens, the
sea coasts, our families, and the loss of our hopes and dreams,
of what we still need to do, to find out, know. Always hungry
in the face of such hauntings.

In the undergrowth of the wood small creatures go about their
business. The moss and lichen, the small delicate ferns, flash
and sparkle with their own movements in the night. Sleeping
birds overhead.

As you enter Fishguard harbour a cargo ship sits on the bottom half-submerged, only the bows, bridge amidships, and the funnel and masts in the stern above water. Seaweed trails from the deck rails and rigging. Once ashore you climb up atop the giant granite cliffs, their edges rich with cowslips, thrift, and orchids in flower. The vast ocean in front of you. Gulls wheeling and squawking in the bright air. This is not a dream. A short distance inland you find standing stones set in small lush wheat fields.

'On certain mornings, as we turn a corner, an exquisite dew falls on our heart and then vanishes. But the freshness lingers, and this, always, is what the heart needs.' (wrote Camus)*

* in *Return to Tipasa*

The beginning of the story

1   The castle was built on a small hill overlooking the river.
    Probably it once commanded the whole valley – chose
    who could pass through the valley, who could come up
    river in boats, who could cross the river at the nearby
    ford. Now it stands empty and the surrounding lands are
    once more scrub and forest. The castle, after all, was only
    built by men and manned by men. And now it is just one
    more feature of the landscape, though maybe more
    passive than most.

2   Parting the leaves you look out on to a sunny meadow
    that slopes down to a small wood with a stream the other
    side.

    A thick wood bordered the meadow with the beech trees'
    branches trailing the ground. The leaves of one tree
    slowly parted and a face appeared.

3   Blue objects flashed before the eyes of the face. As though
    a giant blue boulder dominated the foreground, and all
    else was only a haze. A rounded blue cylinder rising out
    of the earth, or descending from the heavens. There were
    obviously many explanations and interpretations for all
    these stunning phenomena.

4   Late in the morning on a mild and sunny autumn day I
    was in the kitchen. First I made a delicious chocolate
    blancmange, then prepared a bowl of stewed pears made
    even more fragrant by a touch of ground ginger added to
    the boiling syrup before introducing the segments of pear.
    The quiet happiness one feels with such domestic duties
    is perhaps one of the greatest joys of having a home.

    The choice of dishes prepared will obviously signify
    something to a person looking for such things. Whether
    he's right or wrong is of little importance to me.

5   Threading its way along the valley was a string of pack
    horses. One could just make out the small figures of the
    accompanying traders.

    Up here overlooking the valley . . .

    Perhaps they're not traders, or not all traders. Perhaps
    one of them is a magician. How to imagine his clothes?
    that is if he dresses differently from his companions.

    And whether he should be a wizard rather than a
    magician? And whether, rather than these people merely
    being on a journey or trading, there eare more serious
    and more exotic matters in hand? Threats of dragons?
    Threats of invasions by harsh forces, or worse?? Threats
    of the moon disappearing, of tides growing wild and
    ravaging the shores, flooding the valleys?

6   The wind moans about the houses and the last yellowing
    leaves are stripped from the trees. The birds become more
    obvious and seemingly more active in their continual
    search for food.

    Trim the wistaria, tie up the jasmine and honeysuckle,
    re-stake the chrysanthemums, beware the gales. Trim the
    house, all ship-shape. The winter almost upon us.

7   In his pouch the wizard had a small silver box. The box was beautifully engraved with curious designs and the suggested figures of birds, otters, foxes and wild boar. There was no apparent way of opening the box, though it could be opened by the wizard. Inside was a small flint blade and a flower that never faded.

8   A quiet and mild day in early winter. The sunlight in no way clear or bright but somehow there. The garden below my window is all wetness. The last damp yellowing leaves hang from the wistaria. A single half-dead pink rose is the only colour in the flower bed other than the dull browns and greens of the dying leaves surrounding it. On such mornings a similar lethargy fills us.

9   One clear night the wizard stood alone in a small meadow beside the river. The moon was almost full and clearly lit the whole landscape. He placed the silver box on the grass and stepped back a few paces. The box then slowly opened as though of its own accord and, once open, a bright silver light burnt over the whole surface of the box, inside and out. And at the same moment as the silver box opened a blue cylinder of light slowly appeared hovering a few feet above the box. The blue light, at first faint, as the box's own light was, gradually generated more and more power until it was a near-dazzling throbbing humming block of BLUE.

All this happened in silence, though somehow you sensed at the edge of your hearing a small and delicate music almost like the tinkling of glass wind chimes.

After a time that no one could measure or remember the blue cylinder of light began to fade until in the end it was the faintest of outlines, and then disappeared completely. And at the same time the silver box's light also faded and died, leaving the box an almost indistinguishable dark object set in the pale moon-lit grass.

10 A great sadness fills us.

Questions

i) Does the man go mad?
    Does he even commit suicide? (hence a well-rounded drama) or continue a life of quiet suburban despair? (so a well-rounded 'Modern' drama)

ii) Is the wizard murdered soon after this event?
    or several years later?
    or does he lose his powers? slowly or quickly?
    or, the reverse, does he go on to become truly prosperous and renowned for his skills, living to a fine old age?

iii) Late on a summer evening we find ourselves in the leafy suburban streets of some small town whose name we don't as yet know. There is a velvet darkness that brushes our lips and cheeks with great sensuality. This darkness is only broken by the vague pyramids of white light around the rare street lamps, and the opaque yellow glow from some curtained windows where people are still about. The silence hisses and crackles, it is so near complete.

iv) Shrieks of anguish are muffled in blankets.

v)   Do we pour chocolate blancmange over the wise wizard? explaining to him the while that it is a symbolic gesture attacking all he stands for, but that he shouldn't take it personally?

vi) Are we denied peace?
     Not the peace of answers, set ideas, and realised hopes, (stagnation), but the peace to do things we want to do ourselves. To push on, unhindered by jobs, exhaustion, and 'the treacle of fears and evasions'!!??

vii) The man closes his book. Out of his window he knows and sees the seasons change. His guarded optimism is justified by events.

viii) Shrieking statues are suddenly muffled in the public gardens by council workmen. The flowers join in the horrified chorus. 'WHY ME? WHO ME? NOT ME?'

You essai. you o.k.
for Paul Evans

> 'Once again, the philosophy of darkness
> will dissolve above the dazzling sea.'
>> Albert Camus 1948

1

a rock outcrop in the sea

a deserted car standing on the empty road

Gulls shriek in the air above the rock
while below thrift and small orchids flower
in that awesome hush between the waves breaking

The blue leather upholstery of the car is too hot to touch
the sun being that bright and strong today
A neat green cardboard box has been placed on the back seat

The scents of the sea and the coast join
somewhere up there in the sky –
>> A pyramid of light?

Or would you be bored by all this after the first day?
The ground too damp and civilization too far away?
What if it rains and you have to trudge miles to the nearest
shop or pub or public transport to get away from all this, to
have a few decent 'home comforts'?

2 /1900/

Hold the horses! It's Hotel Wolf!
or as they now say, in these modern times,
Wolf Hotel, and since then renamed The Sisson,
Saratoga, Wyoming.

Step inside
to the palm filled lounge and big easy chairs
and just the right soupçon of barbarism.

O cold blooded murderers,
the sweet-hearts and glory of this continent!

'Peaches! Fresh peaches!' cried the two gauchos,
and the little boy, lifting the canvas that covered their fruit cart,
saw only a heap of severed heads.

You do step into the bar, but are rightly nervous beneath your
assured and sporty manner. No tennis courts, here, I'm sorry
to say, only child-like card-games played by unpleasant adults.
I wouldn't stay long if I were you, though I'm not.

3

I turn my back on all that and re-enter
the alchemist's dark chambers
A glass prism is set on the table top
beneath the window and scatters sunlight
in bands of colour 'a marvel to behold'

Books, equipment, and implements are
stacked about the room
all as aids to discover 'the wonders and secrets of nature'
through human invention and curiosity
godlike

a stuffed baby crocodile hangs from the ceiling
the retort glows gold with its fire

Dear Sir,

Your moods of deep depression can weigh heavily on you for several days or more. I can really do very little for you or your state. Such melancholy can take up to 6 years to fade from your heart after the original emotional shock. I would suggest your taking long walks in the countryside and that you try to mix socially as much as is possible.

Signed,
a doctor

4

TO SPELL IT OUT: the barbarity in all its forms,
in the face of which our blundering frailty,
our frail giant-steps.

'This book,' wrote the French Resistance leader Colonel Georges, 'springs from a sadness and a certain amount of disgust at seeing myths take so much precedence over history ... Our truth has no need of mirrors that would exaggerate it.'*

And you, Anna, with your two fierce-looking sisters and, presumably, stories of real hardships and dangers in the now placid Mid-West, or even further west, Kansas maybe. It's different somehow, though I can't explain.

Families on all sides of 'The Water', with their own strengths like islands in the flood, us all sat on top of the roof like a bunch of drenched chickens waiting for the waters to subside and then be submerged again within the family.
It's difficult to explain, warming and frightening at the same time, the love there.

There are the Grand Events, the 'dangerous times' when maybe more than a rightness about a family is needed – though I can't say we live in such times, and, even so, any such dramatic behaviour has to have a base-camp somewhere, n'est-ce pas?   though maybe not

* Colonel Georges (Robert Noireau) – *Le Temps des Partisans*.

228

Paul, you must know it already, but how in the upper left margin of the first page of the manuscript score for *The Fourth of July*, Charles Ives wrote to his copyist –

'Mr Price: Please don't try to make things nice! All the wrong notes are right. Just copy as I have. I want it that way.'

You walk by the sea on a grey February afternoon with your daughter Lucy and a grossly over-enthusiastic dog. On our meeting we remember, though don't talk of it, the obviously lucid and witty conversation we'd had the night before when (somewhat) the worse for drink!

The mistakes, the difficulties . . . these words almost used too much so that they become some sort of totem or excuse, but it all falling, and us too, every whichaway.

In a little frequented corner of the museum we find an old and heavily embroidered trade union banner on display. The gold silk on a dark red velvet background shows a motif of clasped hands, and all of this faded and somewhat the worse for wear too. I can't make out the motto, but it's probably something like 'Strength in Unity' or . . .

Out in the street again we head back towards the beach. The sea really *is* magnificent, a vast sweep of silver-shot slate grey that fades off and up into the white grey of the sky. The chilling sea wind grips our bones.

Just friends

Two men enter a Victorian house in Kensington and view a re-created Arab courtyard and a series of indifferent paintings.

Two men sit by Kensington Round Pond on a chilly autumn day and discuss the birds and animals to be found in cities.

Two men and a woman sit on the swaying top deck of a bus driving along the coast road from Newhaven to Brighton on a November afternoon.

Three men and two women stop to pick up large red-skinned potatoes that had fallen from a farm lorry, and then continue on their walk to see a tree full of herons and a lone kestrel perched on a footpath sign.

Two men walk on a summer evening through the leafy streets of west London and discuss renting a studio.

Two men stride along Hadrian's Wall in March and are met by earnest hikers in orange anoraks and woolly hats.

Two men walk by the sea at night.

Two men in the dark of a hide quietly lift the wooden flaps and observe the mud flats below them, the curlews, dunlins, grey plovers, cormorants, shellducks, redshanks, and herons.

Two men in Essex study an ancient church door with graceful iron work said to be Viking in origin.

Two men wave to one another (figuratively) at a great distance (real) and slowly fade from each other's sight.

Two men write letters to each other and meet, ride a motor-bike, drive in a hired car, and take long train journeys north.

Two men scramble over a recent cliff fall searching for flints and fossils, and then fade in the sea-mist.

One man . . . the lush parks and mute statues.

At this moment I feel close to tears.

A poem for writers

to finally pull the plug on the word machine,
to rise from the chair late one evening
and step back into the quiet and darkness?

The dull white lights of the control-room of
a large hydro-electric dam in Russia
a computer centre in Brighton
the bridge of a giant oil tanker in the Indian Ocean.
Subdued light that reaches every corner
with no variation, tone, or shadow.

To leave the warm desk-light's tent
and step out into the . . .
   'I am just going outside and may be some time, Scottie'

Trains rush through the night,
across country through suburbs past factories oil refineries
  dumps,
the lights from their windows quickly disturbing the dark
  fields and woods
or the railway clutter as they pass through town,
staring in at the bare rooms and kitchens
each lit with its own story that lasts for years and years.
A whole zig-zag path, and the words stumble and fidget
around what has happened.

To walk out one January morning across the Downs
a low mist on the hills and the furrows coated with frost,
the dew ponds iced up.
The cold dry air.
And the sudden excitement when a flock of partridges starts
    up
in front of you and whirrs off and down to the left,
skimming the freshly ploughed fields.

'O ma blessure' groan the trees
with the wounds of a multitude of small boys' penknives.

No, not that –
but the land, the musics, the books
always attendant
amongst the foolish rush and scramble for vainglory,
talk or noise for its own sake, a semblance of energy
but not necessity.

Throw your cap in the air, get on your bike, and pedal off
down hill – it's a joy with no need of chatter,
Hello Chris.

Paralysis

THE TALKING HEAD SPOKE:

> 'Hid in the coarse grasses
> > bee orchids and pyramid orchids,
> > hare bells and   urr . . . (?)
> On the bare hills
> > overlooking the lush hedgerows
> > below . . . (?)'

SPINE SNAPPED
BODY GONE LIMP LUMP
READ ME SCHOLARLY BOOKS
> 'A History of Christianity'
> 'The Journals of Eugene Delacroix'
IN THE TOWN – DON'T STOP – CROWD IN –
WORK WIPE OUT – STUMBLING DEPRESSION,
POVERTY AND ENVY, INSULTS AND EXPLOITATION,
AND OTHER ABSTRACT NOUNS, I.E. IDEAS
slide sideways down and across to:
FLEET SUNK. PLANTATIONS SMASHED,
OVERGROWN, RETURNED TO JUNGLE.
body lying there
dust gathering on the chess pieces
lying there in the still disorder of an open box,
the Baedecker guide to Florence undisturbed on the bookshelf

Midday the gulls squawking on the roof tops
　　in the centre of town,
　　　their giant shadows covering the crowded
　　　streets below as they slide through a blue sky.
Midnight the wind along the cliff path, the sound
　　of waves breaking on the shore, the distant
　　white light of a flashing beacon that
　　interrupts the soft darkness.

ONE BLINK OF MY EYELIDS MEANS 'YES'
TWO BLINKS OF MY EYELIDS MEANS 'NO'.
HEAD SWIVELLING IN GLASS CASE
ON MARBLE PEDESTAL
THE PHILOSOPHER'S STONE.

Bath-time
for Ted Kavanagh & Barry MacSweeney

A motor torpedo boat covered in giant bubbles silently appeared through the early morning mists. It was only when it was almost upon us that we could hear the muffled roar of its engines, and then only faintly.

I have as much knowledge of myself as I do of why I was adrift in that rubber dinghy in the Malay Straits.

All the books and maps and knowledge give us too little, leave large blank spaces, 'terra incognita'.

'. . . citizens who work and find no peace in pain.
                                        I am chains.'

In chained numbness, not confusion, the war boat bears down on me on us where Educated Summaries are not worth a spit in hell. The Cambridge Marxists, with large houses, cars and incomes, can shove it.

'Anarchist Fieldmarshals, Socialist Judges, Dialectic Fuzz, Switched-on Hangmen, and all other benefits of Correct Revolutionary Practice.'

I don't need patronage – I need something else.

The mists clear before the burning sun, the sea empty and flat as a sheet of polished metal. The long day ahead.

Claret

The large grey château isolated in the middle of lawns and pastures that extend beyond reason.

A large dark grey building put to the cruel uses its exterior already suggests.

A Gestapo Headquarters – interrogation rooms and cells – the top window on the left almost exactly half way between the end of the building and the main entrance.

Though this is in my imagination in a sun-filled kitchen in the early afternoon in September.

where such interrogations could equally happen – husband and wife piling up cruelly logical absurdities, complaints, and accusations while the babies cry in the next room.

Monsters & Co.

The top window on the left of a slum tenement seen from a train window passing through east London – Bethnal Green, Stratford, . . .

Stop the train. Step into that room. 'Hello, I am Anthony Barnett, Norway's greatest jazz xylophone player. I saw you through the window. I saw you moving about your room, sitting watching t.v. I had to come to say 'hello', to embrace you. We humans must stick together.'

The film breaks at this point. Crackling noises and smoke pour from the improvised projection room. The village priest rushes out threatening the noisy audience to be quiet or else . . . If we sit quiet and still we will be allowed to see the rest of *Sabu the Elephant Boy* with French sub-titles.

Text for two posters by Ian Brown / poster 1

It's the vase of tulips and a mirror trick, though this time the
vase is not set between facing mirrors but between a mirror
and a painting of a mirror with a vase of tulips, and this in
turn photographed.

It's the beautifully printed exhibition note in front of a Korean
bowl that has been placed on burnt umber hessian. It quotes
Bernard Leach's praise of the 'unselfconscious asymmetry'
of Korean potters, and how nothing in nature is symmetri-
cal, but everything is asymmetrical, a nose not perfectly
straight, the eyes not perfectly level.

It's those dreams of perfection, 'the man of your dreams',
'woman of your dreams', 'the budgie of your dreams', 'your
dreams come true' to a jarring chorus of cash registers and
half-stifled moans.

Again and again and again and again, and the months and
years glide by hardly noticed so heavy and dull is the
obsession.

to raise your head for one moment clear of this

        skies and clouds ahead
        and the fields and cities below
        as you fly through the sunlight

And below, not looking up,
'Are you going to see the new gorillas?' he asked as we
walked briskly towards the Jardin des Plantes.

A cold dry day in January with mist on the Downs,
  frost on the furrows and ice on the ponds.
A flock of partridges suddenly starting up in front of me,
  and whirring off to the left skimming the ploughed fields.

but André Gide wrote: 'The strange mental cowardice which makes us perpetually doubt whether future happiness can equal past happiness is often our only cause for misery; we cling to the phantoms of our bereavements, as if we were in duty bound to prove to others the reality of our sorrow. We search after memories and wreckage, we would like to live the past over again, and we want to reiterate our joys long after they are drained to the dregs.

I hate every form of sadness, and cannot understand why trust in the beauty of the future should not prevail over worship of the past.'

/poster 2

SLEEPERS AWAKE
from the 'sensible life' whose only passion is hatred

A red and black pagoda towers above the chestnut trees
in a Royal Botanic Garden
The lush greens of south London back-gardens
O summer nights when trembling with that ecstasy
our bodies sweat and flood one another's

Burst forth – sun streams forth – light –
all doors and windows magically thrown open
a hot lush meadow outside
with dark green woods at its edges

turn it another way
These are insistences not repetitions
or the repetitions are only the insistence on

and it all crowds in:

'Nostalgia for the life of others . . . Whereas ours, seen
from the inside, seems broken up. We are still chasing
after an illusion of unity.'
'Separation is the rule. The rest is chance . . .'*

which way to step?

and the dull brutality of monsters as they grind the bones
'forbidden to delight one's body, to return to the truth of
    things'*

* Albert Camus – *Notebooks*

The clouds part, your hand reaches through – yes
the glow and light in us, our bodies

And below around us – the flint customs house at Shoreham,
the call of a cuckoo as we climb up-hill to the Stalldown stone
   row,
the wild moor about, and from its edges
the churches, cathedrals, ancient and beautiful things.

Talking to myself

The sweet qualities of our dreams without which . . .

How the wind blows and our hearts ache to follow
the hazardous route the winds follow

                6 million Russians
                6 million Jews
                2 million Poles
                1 million Serbs
                Gypsies and others

The fern cabinet

'in that enchanted calm which they say lurks
          at the heart of every commotion'

the dream look on an angel's half turned face

a faint cloud passes and
the distant landscape is precise in every detail

to hold to 'a wide and hospitable mind', a generous spirit

to 'walk joyfully throughout all the world
and answer that of god in everyman'

a keel set for all the storms
and onshore the carefully jointed and polished mahogany,
the small forest of delicate green plants trembling

we die alone, lie alone

                    ('nor be in bodies lost')

though 'There are no impervious skins or membranes in
  nature, no "outlines". Nothing is ever quite isolate.'

two flights of geese come in from the east, the sun behind
them, flying low over the sea and across the dunes to the
moorland beyond and the still water there. The sparkle of the
sea with the wind rising, the sharp marram grass, the purple
heather.

'I still bathe me in eternal mildness of joy'

(Quotations from Herman Melville, J.L. Borges, George Fox,
John Dryden, Antony Lopez, and Herman Melville.)

Dream Quilt

Nautical business

Growing up in that south coast town in the 1920s and '30s — there was really little choice for the boy. At the age of 14 he joined the Royal Navy. After the tough and rigorous training at Portsmouth he was sent to sea. His first ship was on patrol in the Yangtse River. The young sailor's duty was to keep watch at night in the bows. He was there with a long pole to push the bodies that floated down-stream away from the ship. When a very young child he had accompanied his grandfather, who was a shepherd, for whole days on the Downs. As far as the eye could see the hills were speckled white with the flocks.

Booth's Bird Museum

The long grasses and reeds at the edge of the marsh thrashed and sighed as the wind got up.

A duck punt silently slid out onto the mere. The hunter lay prone on the punt's bottom, his breath white in the winter air. Small white clouds puffed into the dawn.

The deafening explosion of the punt gun brought a rain of fowls that flopped into the water. Expertly gathered by the dogs the birds were hurried to the museum to be stuffed and placed in a naturalistic setting.

The smell of highly polished linoleum and slowly leaking radiators.

Mosquito nets

He had passed through the jungle and left the river region far behind. The expedition was now camped close to a native village out on the grasslands. The veldt stretched off flat and endless whichever way he looked. Here and there an odd stunted scrubby tree survived somehow.

The other members of the expedition searched for insects and small mammals. His own contribution was to make a study of the ways of the village and the language of this hitherto remote tribe. He found that he had to continually reconsider all the assumptions he'd made about the native customs and habits. It was both a stimulating and a troubling experience for him.

Under his mosquito nets the explorer dreamed that night of his young children sleeping, sprawled in their beds at 'home'.

Woolly rhinoceros

In the August of 1833 Charles Darwin arranged to leave *The Beagle* at El Carmen in Patagonia and ride overland to Buenos Aires where he would rejoin the ship. During his crossing of the Pampas he had to visit the camp of the notorious General Rosas and his army of gauchos. It was necessary for Darwin to obtain a pass from the General to allow him to safely continue his journey. Rosas was at that time embarked on a campaign of genocide against the region's indians. It was later that he became the bloody dictator of the Argentine.

It is curious that in none of his stories does Borges mention this chance meeting of the great theoretician and a ruthless practitioner of the theory of survival of the fittest.

Dream bed

The two athletes were running side by side across the country-side in perfect unison. It looked almost as if they were loping rather than running. Maybe they were ballet dancers and this a rigorous training session for all the 'grands jetés' in *L'après-midi d'un faune*. When they reached the narrow plank foot-bridge across a wide stream – this was somewhere near Winchester – they reluctantly had to run one behind the other.

On the other side of the stream stood a small potting-shed in the midst of some trees. Someone had foolishly shelled the two hard-boiled eggs clutched by the runner. When they were placed in the coarse lunch sack in the shed there was no way they could avoid being coated with dirt and hairs.

'Very interesting,' said the doctor after a significant pause.

Purple sheets

Low clouds trailed across the mountain slopes, obscuring the ridge and peaks above. It was late one afternoon in December. At this hour the forests appeared a dull black and the sea below a smoky light grey. As dusk approached you could see the regular flash of the lighthouse on the distant headland of Point Reyes.

At this time there were two lighthouse keepers on duty. The head-keeper was a solitary man. He had never married, and with his father dead the only family he had left was a mother who lived in a far away country town. In a way his present life on these lonely cliffs perfectly suited his temperament. The assistant-keeper was an equable and happily married man. He and his wife lived in a snug cottage that sheltered in a hollow behind the lighthouse. Each night they slept in each other's arms. Their bed had purple flannel sheets with dark blue pillows, but that's another story.

Hommage à Beatrix Potter

'Show   no mercy,' purred the ginger cat. 'That's the
way   it goes,'
'But ... but ...' stammered the bewildered pet lover. 'Are
you sure? I mean ... well ...'
His question was interrupted by the sharp noise of two mice
hacking the plaster food in the doll's house.
The brandishing of a poker doesn't solve it.
Maybe painting watercolours of mushrooms or breeding prize
sheep solves it.
But pokers, rolling-pins, sticks, flower-pots, and even sharp
teeth don't solve it, frightening though they may be at that
moment.
The onions fall from my large pocket handkerchief and roll
down the garden path.

Climbing party

Sheltering in a jagged rock outcrop near the summit of Glyder Fawr Mr Evans and Mr Harwood snorted with irritation.

Below them – on the saddle of the ridge between Glyder Fach and Glyder Fawr – their companions floundered like beached seals.

'What's the matter with them?'

'Why don't they get a move on? No back bone!'

These and similar disparaging and irritable remarks were muttered at the slowness and general lack of effort and determination by their friends.

Little did Evans and Harwood realize, or want to realize, that Mr Bailey and the Davies brothers were in fact pinned to the bare rocky ground by the force of the gale. Their negligence in not being properly equipped with crampons and ice-axes was now painfully obvious.

Eventually, by traversing the wild boulders and scree beside and below the Devil's Kitchen, the party was able to descend from the heights just as dusk was falling. They made it down just in time and were certainly lucky in meeting a lone climber who'd shown them the last part of the route.

Later, as they walked in the moonlight along the shores of Llyn Ogwen, Evans remembered that 1765 journal entry of Thomas Gray's:

> 'The mountains are ecstatic, and ought to be visited in pilgrimage once a year. None but those monstrous creatures of God know how to join so much beauty with so much horror.'

Once back at the cars the party divided – the Davies brothers leaving for Bala, and Evans, Harwood and Bailey returning to Waunfawr.

That evening in the near deserted dining room of the Royal Hotel, Caernarfon, after several gin and tonics, after a reasonable dinner and two bottles of Mouton Cadet, after eyeing the young waitresses and remarking on the same, the three gentlemen – approaching their middle years – rose from the table. All that remained on that sharp January night was the habitual negotiations as to who should have the unique hotwaterbottle in their rented cottage. Such are the subtle pleasures and true exhilarations of life.

'A man without faults is like a mountain without crevasses. He doesn't interest me,'* thought Harwood that night in bed as he clutched the hotwaterbottle.
'Most enjoyable,' said Bailey sleepily.

* René Char – *Feuillets d'Hypnos*.

Birthday Boy

Many years ago Bill Butler said that your birthday was the one day in the year when you should do exactly as you like. I immediately took this advice to heart, realizing the pure pleasure and sanity of having one completely selfish day free from all obligation to others.

Today, the 6th of June, 1984, is my 45th birthday. The sequence of my pleasures:

Waking into a fine summer morning with the sun shining and blue skies over Brighton. A cup of coffee and lying in bed reading Jocelyn Brooke's book of poems *The elements of death*.

A long walk on the South Downs between Berwick and Eastbourne, taking the most roundabout and charming route, botanising and idling on the way.*

A telephone call from my son Rafe to wish me a happy birthday.

Dinner.**

A concert by the Chilingirian Quartet in which they played Bartok's wild, witty, yet very moving duos for two violins, as well as two very pleasant Mozart pieces – the trio in E flat for clarinet, viola and piano, and the piano quartet in G minor. The quartet was joined for these last two pieces by Andrew 'suitably dishevelled' Marriner (clarinet) and Clifford 'elegant to a fault' Benson (piano).

The day finishes with an agreeable late night conversation and glass of scotch with Adrian Kendon. And so to bed.

It would have been nice to have shared some of these pleasures with another person, but such are my circumstances that this was not possible or, rather, not the case.

* * *

(*)How to describe a summer's day in the Sussex countryside? Such an account, it seems, can't help but appear wayward and dull, the whole pleasure being somehow 'low key' and near indescribable. And yet that pleasure is one of the most acute and important in my life. I'm not just talking about the vague delights of 'Nature' and 'the countryside', but about a very particular countryside, that of south east England, something very special for me. But even so, how real can such a subtle obsession and love be for those who don't know this landscape?

I take the train from Brighton to Berwick. It's a lovely bright sunny morning with a soft warm breeze and small white clouds flying through the skies. From Berwick station I turn south and follow the lane for a mile or so down into Berwick village. Along the banks and hedgerows – blue shepherd's purse, tall rich yellow buttercups, purple clover, pink and white campions, herb robert, and the dirty white lace of cowparsley. And behind the hedges – the lush greens of the meadows and wheatfields. And above – the repeated cries and warbles of a scatter of skylarks.

At Berwick village I stop for a beer and sandwich in the garden of the Cricketer's Arms. Surrounded by flowers how strange that one's eyes focus on one thing – the white paper doily on the plate – that triggers memories of past private worlds. No, not Jocelyn Brooke's bar of transparent green soap nor Proust's madeleine, but a paper doily.

In Berwick church – a mainly Saxon building sited on a prehistoric mound – I'm surprised to find paintings by Duncan Grant and Vanessa Bell. The walls, rood screen, altar and even the pulpit are decorated with their work. A nativity scene is but one of the many subjects chosen. A virgin surrounded by Sussex shepherds and young boys with 1940s haircuts, a view of the Downs as a background. I'm doubly surprised as the paintings are quite good and not the usual mess of pastel colours and poor draughtsmanship I've come to expect from, for example, Duncan Grant.

I continue south towards Alfriston, walking along a narrow path down through a field of wheat then up through barley on the opposite slope of this shallow valley. My hands brush the ears of corn as I walk, but I'm absurdly distracted by imagining Alfriston will be crowded with coach parties of Midlanders. All of this appears completely foolish as, when I do walk through Alfriston, all I meet are a handful of elderly tourists, all quite innocent and well-meaning. Fear and snobbery obviously go hand in hand in my case.

Once beyond the village I take the path south-east across the fields and then up onto the ridge of the Downs just above *The Long Man of Wilmington*. The glaring white of the chalk track and the call of the cuckoo in the spinneys below. I then walk east along the ridge across the short-cropped turf, pausing at the barrow above the *Man* to admire the pale blue flowers of the wild thyme. Suddenly two army helicopters roar overhead. It's the 'D-Day' anniversary. I'd forgotten.

I then descend from the ridge across the steep pastures towards Folkington to visit my orchid track. It's become almost a ritual. Each birthday I come here to visit this secret and magic place. But everything is disappointingly late this year. The cowslips are still in flower and I can only find five common spotted orchids, and them barely pink with their flowers not yet open. I lie back in the long grass and close my eyes. The warmth of the sun on my face, a blackbird singing in a nearby hawthorn bush, the rustle of the leaves in the breeze. Pure heaven with a few erotic trimmings.

Eventually I have to leave and take the path south to Jevington, then up Willingdon Hill onto the bare high Downs again. The long sweeping views – the thick green Weald to the north, the cliff-tops and sea to the south. The sweep of the coast east to Hastings. Reluctantly I continue across the tops and down into Eastbourne and the inevitable late afternoon train back to Brighton.

(**)Dinner was a slight disappointment. Not the hoped for meal that would combine excellent French cooking with good wines, but egg and chips at the Lewes Road Diner. A slight blot, but . . .

John Butler to the rescue

Greater generosity hath no man than to let a friend row his dory.

Not for me 'the stream of consciousness ramblings of an agitated mind' that Mr Berkson's reviewer comments on. Rather the civilized delights of gliding across the water in a truly elegant skiff or dory. To pull on a fine pair of oars and effortlessly slide through the water. To have them sweep clear of the water and swing back sweetly dripping ready for the next stroke. To dip them in the water and pull again on towards the small sandy island, the haunt of seals and herons.

Such a range of pleasures. *John Biglin in a Single Scull*, that rosy-cheeked determined gentleman portrayed by Thomas Eakins; or Monet's lazy and sociable driftings down the Seine; or the satanic Alfred Jarry in his racing shell. What need of a nobler lineage?

These summer pleasures – so distant from the wintry past. Almost forgotten the low mist over the frozen river and the ice encrusted willows on the opposite bank. A man in a long black coat crossing over as though dancing to the irregular reports of the cracking ice. A secret messenger or a fleeing refugee? A host of possible stories. And further south, with the thaw well on its way, the night ferry chugs across the estuary. The distracted lover or an anguished spy walks the rail, blankly staring at the lights of passing freighters.

No, this is long past and summer is truly here. In the immaculate lifeboat station the coxwain John Butler can untie his cork life-jacket and go home to his family.

Almost blinded by the sunlight he steps from the building and gazes at the surrounding mountains that slide into a glittering sea.

Domino Champion

My grandfather – that is my mother's father – suddenly dropped dead late one summer in his garden. He was over 80 and had had no previous illnesses. There could really be no better way to die. To suddenly be struck down in the middle of all those roses and dahlias that he loved and treasured so much.

From this distance he can be said to have had a hard but happy life, As a young man he worked in a boot and shoe factory – one of the few choices a working man living in the Midlands had in those days, that or the mines. Intent on 'getting on' and learning his trade, once a week after finishing work he used to walk the ten miles to Leicester to attend evening classes on the leather trade and shoe design.

Eventually he and his cousin started their own shoe factory in a small terrace house. In the two rooms upstairs the 'clickers' worked cutting out the leather uppers and the women machining them together. In the downstairs the leather soles were stamped out and then nailed and sewn to the uppers. The 'office' consisted of a 6 foot by 4 foot cubicle at the head of the stairs. Everyone in the family worked in the factory.

During the 1930s the factory made boots and shoes for the big shoe shops, and by the late 40s had expanded into the next door house, using the back garden for storing the hides. By the time his sons and daughters took over the factory it was truly prospering. My grandfather, though, never retired. Right up to his death he would light the factory boilers early each morning, tend them and potter round the finishing room for the rest of the day.

My 'Uncle' Ernest, who had a larger factory a few streets away, was even more successful. He had married my grandfather's sister, Hannah, and even in the 30s he was doing well. But despite his success he was regarded by the rest of the family as a disgrace. His 'crime' had been making boots with cardboard soles for the Republican Government during the Spanish Civil War. The disgrace was probably more to do with ideas of honesty and good craftsmanship than anything political.

My mother and I used to visit Aunt Hannah, even though such visits were disapproved of by my grandparents. I remember the front-room with its cabinet of Uncle Ernest's ivory curios. The strings of elephants, of course, and a series of balls, one inside another, all carved from one piece of ivory. But most of all I remember an ivory pagoda about two foot high that stood on a table, I think, the other side of the room. It had little doors you could open, and inside the bottom door was a carved statue of the Buddha. It was beautiful and, for me at the age of five or six, a magical thing.

I've no idea where it is now nor who owns it – but I still think about it. Just as I still think about my grandfather fifteen years after his death. A dear man whose great joys were the prize roses and dahlias he grew in the summer, the magnificent chrysanthemums in the autumn, and the vine he tended in a small hothouse. A gentle man who during the war used to send us each year a bunch of black grapes in a shoe box.

Announcement: Swallows don't hibernate in mud at the bottom of ponds

On the 12th of February, 1778, the first truly scientific British naturalist, Gilbert White, wrote to his friend Daines Barrington:

'Besides, it does not appear from experiment that bees are in any way capable of being affected by sounds: for I have often tried my own with a large speaking-trumpet held close to their hives, and with such an exertion of voice as would have hailed a ship at the distance of a mile, and still these insects pursued their various employments undisturbed, and without showing the least sensibility or resentment.'

The all-hearing bees happily ignored the Rev. White, just as the runnerbeans ignored Darwin's trombone playing. The bees kept buzzing and the beans growing while navigators and neighbours were alarmed by strange unexplained sounds drifting over the horizon.*

A group of ladies passed along a narrow footpath the other side of the hedge, chattering loudly. The scent of honeysuckle and roses sweetening the air. They entered the garden and went into the house for tea. Bursts of talk and laughter floating through the open windows long after.

*It is curious how often those we cherish most have such foibles, even pure wrong-headedness. The strange racial theories about the peasantry, for example, to be found amongst all the excellent writings on the countryside by W.H. Hudson.

Malaysia Dreaming

The minesweeper was anchored close to the shore. With the war over the crew couldn't see why they should continue patrolling these waters. It was therefore up to the captain to keep their minds off such dangerous thoughts. The result was that days were filled with busy and pointless tasks. Discipline was tightened. Some sailors, who had dived into the sea to cool off, were even threatened with court-martial for desertion. And that was no idle threat. Lieutenant Mortimer Cat had his orders and resolutely intended to carry them out, correctly and efficiently.

The lieutenant, who strangely was to become a professor of literature in later years, gazed at the shore. The green palms swayed in an offshore breeze. The white beach was near dazzling in the mid-afternoon brightness. Of course he'd heard rumours there was some new 'show' afoot, but that was all too far from his immediate concerns. When orders came they came. Not that one didn't have one's opinions, but . . .

No, if anywhere his thoughts strayed back to HMS King Alfred, the shore base where he'd done his officer training, and Showell Styles, that curious gunnery officer he'd met there. Recent gossip had it that Lieutenant-Commander Styles had been excelling in his eccentricity. The latest was that, while outfitting armed merchant navy vessels (D.E.M.S.*) in the port of Haifa in Palestine, Styles had climbed Mount Jebel Kafr Manda in full dress whites along with sword, medals, and all. This costume was apparently in deference to the local Arab

* Defensively Equipped Merchant Ships.

etiquette that one dressed according to one's rank. That was all very well, thought Cat, but just not on, a bit off in fact.

He was roused from his reverie by the strong smell of oil rags and the clunk of boots on the iron rungs of a companion-way as the chief petty officer emerged from the engine-room. But these immediate surroundings faded only too quickly as he drifted again into memories of that wintry seaside town. The black statues of dead queens staring out to sea at dusk and the lights coming on in the top floor windows of those long white terraces. Obscure members of exiled royal families in their overheated and cluttered rooms. The shouts of green-grocers dismantling their displays at the end of the day. Beautifully arranged pyramids of apples, oranges and pears, cauliflowers and leeks, all edged with a line of those red string bags of assorted nuts. And always around the corner the worn boarding houses in small dark squares.

And then? Years ahead an overgrown tombstone in Lewes Road Cemetery? A stained marble cross and anchor inscribed:
> 'Faithful below he did his duty,
> And now he's gone aloft!'

Tofu in Carolina

The story was meant to begin with two dragons lazily flying south from their mountain home. They were to have been passing over Tremadoc Bay on their way to Harlech when a witch appeared. The story revolved around the little known fact that when dragons open their wings at a full moon gold dust falls out. The witch was to be intent on capturing the dragons to brush their gold from them.

But this tale is interrupted by visions of people who die before their time or suffer long and painful illnesses. Though all this seems equally remote to the healthy and vigorous souls. Whatever it is happens out there, is beyond real belief.

One of the dragons was called Bronwyn and the other Paul, her young brother. The witch was known as Rita of Talsarnau. That the story couldn't be told disappointed all these characters, especially as they all had rather exciting parts. Paul was to have been caught in a dark net by Rita. Bronwyn tried to rescue him by various means, but failed. She then would have called in her friend Hugo the giant and together, using a number of disguises, they would have tried again. Maybe they would have been successful; or maybe all three would have had to be rescued from a black cave by Mr Bailey and a party of his students out sketching rocks and trees. There are so many possible endings. But one way or another they all finish with the death of Rita the witch of Talsarnau.

It's grim in ways you don't expect. Dogged by all the obvious pain and fears – yet you shut them out. The stories, if you suspend your disbelief, are not lulling.

'No,' she said, driving fast down the winding mountain road, 'that mode is basically uninteresting. It lacks real energy.'

But beyond the immediate? What's over that horizon? or around the curve? Such dreamy questions have an edge to them, a hard bone below the soft fur. And the wonder. The gold dust falling from the sky like a gentle snow. An older woman taking two steps in a hospital ward.

The Land of Counterpane

The toys were all ready. The faded but resolute general, the mountie with movable arms, the nurse, and the three sheep. They all set off along the maze of narrow rounded valleys that criss-crossed the green and mauve eiderdown. Their journey was not to be without adventure – the sick child was sure of that as he spoke out loud their conversations. The sheep with three legs kept falling over so had to be propped between the other two sheep or set against a suitable slope. The path was like those that wind from the crest of the Downs south to the sea. Bare hills and small copses set deep in the combes.

They bravely struggled on. They would fulfil their vague and continually changing mission and then return home. When dusk overtook them they started to make camp. They soon fell asleep around the campfire, but were suddenly awakened by a giant hand that descended from the sky. Though plucked from their world they soon settled into their new home, a box on the bedside table. The curtains were drawn and the child was soon asleep.

In the next-door house the child's two friends were also asleep. The boy, who is King of the Birds, can understand everything they say, lies curled up clutching his blue blanket. The girl, who is Queen of the Insects, sprawls in her bed, her arms and legs thrown out, fearless. One of their parents enters the bedroom and stands watching them as they sleep. It's as though he's trying to make time stand still, to somehow fix forever this scene in his memory. As tenuous as trying to engrave the colours of the sky in one's mind. The silver and

gold over the sea seen late one afternoon looking from the
Roman Steps west across to Bardsey. Moments that go beyond
joy or tenderness into some other land that's beyond any
words.

> 'I was a giant great and still
> That sits upon the pillow-hill,
> And sees before him, dale and plain,
> The pleasant land of counterpane.'*

* Robert Louis Stevenson – *A Child's Garden of Verses*

Monster Masks
and other creatures

Faded ribbons around the lost bundle now being devoured by moths

Homage to William Strang

Late on a hot summer's night in Central Park

> (At this point creaking noises are heard as a faded and flaking cloth backdrop is unrolled showing a star filled sky and crude silhouettes of palm trees – a touch incongruous, but . . .)

two adults skip through the planned woodland to the children's playground where they vigorously swing on the swings, laughing and talking all the time.

> (Various constellations of white stars are set on the midnight blue – graphic fictions of the bear, Orion the hunter, the ladle, the plough. A special effects machine is working hard in the wings pumping out a soft humid air to match the scene.)

After their games they amble somewhat aimlessly across the park towards the streets and buildings. Where next with the romantic rush? that will possibly end in dissatisfaction and second thoughts in a dishevelled bed in an airless apartment?

'Dawn approaches, the sky lightens appropriately' read the stage directions.

* * *

A clear sky suddenly appears when I close my eyes.
There are no clouds on this day.
A monoplane slowly crosses the sky, returns, circles,
then goes off on its way.

A woman enters in loose thin pants.
Clouds, small white clouds appear,
and cross from left to right.

A spin of the compasses that stride off
to Cologne, Hanover, and Berlin.

The dream on the close cropped turf of the chalk ridge
blurs, then fades into telephones and posted objects.

* * *

A 14th century Italian painter, who specializes in gold leaf, appears at this point with his apprentices. There is much clattering of paint pots. Trestles are set up, and pigments are ground in the mortars. Bright sunlight streams through the high windows onto this scene of noisy industry that, as the days progress, will subside into the sounds of brush strokes and intermittent groans as men shift their cramped bodies.

Days, months, even years, pass all for that day when the patron will enter and gasp with wonder at the finished work.

Angels cluster and rustle just to the side of my vision.

Years later . . .

* * *

sun streams through the window
onto the table

there is fruit in the bowl on the table
and flowers in the vase

the bare white walls gleam
with that reflected sunlight

You open the window
The pleasure of summer days slides by
unnoticed –
as though timeless – the days mingling

The trees rustle and sigh
as the wind comes up

I touch your shoulder
with my lips
and you then turn to me smiling

The vines are doing well this year
The house stands firm, clear and fresh
as it was hoped
Our embraces seal the knot

* * *

the arrogant woman in the large red hat
and bright green dress stares out of her gilt frame,
a book held limply in her left hand

LIBER GENERATIONIS IHESU CHRISTI FILII DAVID FILII
ABRAHAM

                              son of David son of Abraham
A black crow's feather lies on the moor's coarse grass,
is picked up and carefully taken to a house many miles away.

A white and blue and red feathered archangel
tramples the dragon and opens the loving scroll

Children joyfully rush about gathering the short grey and
brown feathers they've discovered in the hill pasture
happily ignorant of history and the death involved

Her pale and flushed face aches with tension.
Anger and violence seethe like maggots
beneath her glazed refinement.
For one moment – to get up and stride about the room –
will she? No, she remains seated on a hard high-backed chair.
The question of where vanity and obsession meet or divide
or . . .

'Suffer little children to come unto thee'

*　*　*

A starling's breast crowded with lustrous stars
set on a black varnished night
and the angels all a-flutter

And, washing the whitewash from our hands, we remember
that Henry the Third's 'favourite decorative motif, in both his
castles and his palaces, was gold stars on a green background
. . . Work, he commands, must be *decens, pulcher, sumptuosus.'*

the sound of children laughing outside

Then gusts of rain and wind and
a blur of colours signals the arrival of the rainbow door
We step through into a meadow of long grass
scattered with dandelions and dog daisies

A 13th century ceiling meets Schubert meets
a glass of chilled white wine and a ripe peach

*　*　*

[The Progress of the Walk]

blackbird's song
skylark's trill
cuckoo's call

lush woodland
wheatfield
re-entering the trees

an aeroplane circling
naked lovers

a blue butterfly
a small fragment of decorated pottery
The End:

A child's view of railways
for Rowan Harwood

The railway station is shut for the night.
The trains stand silent beside the dark platforms.
The train drivers have all gone home
   and are now asleep in their beds.
The gates are locked against a burglar
   who might steal chocolate cake
   and lemons from the buffet,
   or tickets from the ticket office.
The small shed is also padlocked
   where all the parcels and letters are kept
   ready for the morning trains.
Another shed has been kindly provided for passengers
   to sleep in while they wait for trains,
   and this too has been locked against the same
   possible burglar.
Though the railway policewoman will go and get
   the lemon back from the burglar – at night.

The lost children wander amongst the heavy
   railway clutter talking in their sleep.
A magic black cat will solve all the problems
   and then they can build a new world
   and begin a new story.
Tea and coffee will be served to all the animals.

Hand from an Exeter cloud

Yes, now the night closes in. Yes, now the fireworks display over the cathedral has ended. What now? The single bed in the 'guest room', the copies of Jules Laforgue's *Oeuvres completes* at your head, distant traffic on the nearby main road?

'Is this something new?' asks the clerk sarcastically.
Not exactly . . .

Dreams of children's voices heard the other side of a thicket. Dark green tunnels through the bushes and undergrowth. And later the next day leafing through an exhibition catalogue of Elizabethan miniatures – the sudden shock and recognition on seeing one titled 'Man clasping a hand from a cloud'.

For the photographer Kurt Hutton

The dreadful loneliness
that cuts short all talk, all words.
Men and women walking the night streets,
snow on the lawns and ice in the gutters.
And one person walks from one point to another,
then, after a brief stay, back again
walled in by the cold, the heart, the tongue.

The white hills are criss-crossed
with tracks – animals, birds, and humans.
Such clear marks of time and existence.
And in the hollow the makings of sad posies
– old man's beard, rosehip, and yarrow.

As though planets of ice roll through space
in slow motion while the fathers of previous years
lie under frozen soil, bereft of that warmth so dear to us.

Monster masks

Masked monsters stalk the land

        Grey Monsters Gain the Day
                  .

'Trust me' said the monster. Who should, why should anyone
trust the monster? as he delicately and handsomely
dances the steps of his greedy desire. A personal tango
(with complications).

'stroke my fur, sniff my scent'

        Running naked in the rain
        Runnng round in pulsing circles
        in the clearing

touch me touch me don't touch me don't touch me
touch me touch me
don't touch me don't touch me touch me touch me
don't touch me don't touch me

        In a bare and spacious room
        filled with light – the windows
        opening onto early summer
        The quiet, and clarity of thought.
        Descartes and the 18th century meet
        the wolf boy of Aveyron (c1800),
        the Noble 'Savage of Aveyron'.

From a narrow window the minotaur gazes down on the lights of the city. On such evenings the loneliness almost overwhelms him, trapped and hidden in his labyrinth. The maze as much a protection for him as a trap for his victim.

The beast within

aped by cheap comedians and actors,
nervous commercial ventures, on a fine knife edge,
feed some need

Beauty and the Beast.

Alpine mastiffs reanimating a distressed traveller*

When you step through the rainbow door do you find yourself
on a bare mountain slope with the first winter snow falling?
possibly even in the middle of a blizzard crouching
behind a rock face for shelter? Or is it
into a deep meadow scattered with flowers and birdsong?
Not so much a matter of heaven and hell, but . . .

Civilized pursuits are abandoned in the busy rush.
The heaven of playing chess, of country walks and
mountain climbing, of good company and food and drink,
music and books. The true heaven of being loved and loving.
But the 'Busy Rush' rules, and 'Tenderness' is shown the door.
As these abstract nouns lumber by we head into the ice.

But the distressed traveller, dusting snow from his fur mittens,
struggles free from this particular avalanche, patting the heads
of the helpful and friendly mastiffs. The Tyrolean monks
    approach
and once more the wolf pelt covering on his gloves has proved
    its efficacy.
At such times, like a gleaming ikon before his eyes, he
    imagines
walking along a seashore late in the afternoon with his loved
    one.

* Title courtesy of Sir Edwin Landseer's 1820 painting

The Heart and Hand, North Road, Brighton
for Ann

And they took Bran's head to the royal hall at Gwales. Eighty years they spent at Gwales and they could not remember having spent a happier or more joyful time. But one day Heilyn son of Gwynn opened the door 'we must not open' and looked out at the Bristol Channel and Cornwall, and as he did so they all became conscious of every loss, of every ill that had befallen them, as if it had all just happened.

And then shift to . . . ? shift to opera? why not? King Priam, Hector and Paris bathing their hands in the blood of Patroclus' hacked body. Erotic corpse fondling. Gnawed. (Courtesy of M. Tippett.)

Then side step to Byron clawing the heart from Shelley's burning body.

All this, and then one night running through the rain along the narrow streets. I stumble into a pub and see you there, an 'old friend'. The evening keeps rolling, onto and into the drinking club, to lying in bed with you, us sleeping like precocious children in a room overlooking the city's centre.

Such accidents or the gods again.

And at dawn walking back through the deserted streets – the relief of having shared such tenderness, to be chosen. The silky colours of the morning's sky, pale greens and blues. And the street cleaners quietly talking as they start their work.

But yes, I love my elegant footwear, neat haircuts, a good tweed jacket and tight jeans (aging poet turned artistic country gent?), a black knit tie and light blue shirt. Robin Blaser, you honey.

My heart leaps into your hands. 'Those years the happiest they'd known.' How many of us left? It's all out there falling around and us too. And didn't he say somewhere, the sexual act is the 'nearest' we can get to feeling completely secure, to being totally alive, timeless.

Desert phone

My heart melts at the sound of your voice,
at the sight of your words.

Our long history on small scraps of paper.

We cross the river and then, in the willow grove beyond,
prepare for the next stage,
go straight on even, our clothes still dripping with water.

And later
as though lost on the plain,
scrub bushes, canyons, the hot flat desert
with rolling blond hills on its edges
and the arid mountains beyond.

How did we get here? we ask ourselves,
too hot to cling to each other for safety
and instead, dazed, seem to wander in circles.

No wise words, only a vague hope and trust
that waves like a mirage, falters
with the light breeze at evening time.

I can talk of your nakedness or your fire
but I won't.

What is the thin green line on the horizon?
Tree tops that line a cool steep valley?
another river?

The beams in the house are rotting, need replacing.
Too much weight? The burning blue
sky pressing down.

Coat of arms on wall in ancient city

Bears dance to the music, slowly, awkwardly
in the grand piazza.
A thin but sufficient chain keeps them in place.

Grotesque beasts look on,
beasts cobbled together from various spare parts
and men's strange imaginations.
Is that a crocodile or an eroded dragon?
A winged lion or a sphinx?
All the world's plunder cobbled together.

Mists coat the lagoon this evening
as the ferry passes a low barge,
a pleasure launch and a small naval landing craft
on the flat waters.

In the palazzo an evening of decadence
is about to begin and the end is expectantly planned
for systematic and cold debauchery,
whips and black undergarments,
a series of calculated and delightful humiliations,
pains and pleasures.

Has the icon, looted from Cyprus, seen it all before?
The resigned virgin with child
cluttered with necklaces and improbable crowns.
A look of indifference is all we see.
She may sternly pity our fate, or
not even know it. Tough luck!
We'll get by.

We board the throbbing steamer.
Here come the bears hurrying from their last
   evening performance and just in time.
'All aboard' someone shouts in Italian.
The splendours fade behind us as
we're cloaked in a sweet velvet darkness.
Ahead is the unseen landing stage,
the sound of crickets and frogs
and a bored bus driver calling to a friend.

The bears troop off and disappear into the night.
Their plans remain ambiguous.

Picture postcards and an object
for John Giorno

The grey ochre building seen vaguely
in sunlight. Trees in foreground.
Mediterranean even. Calm warm surface
with the tremble of nerves, hysteria, beneath.

To rush into the palm filled lounge to
wicker chairs and tables, and cool tiles underfoot
– hotels with strutting peacocks screeching in the grounds –
and then stop, twisting and turning, and out.

No, the calmly worried look of the madonna
in a cracked fresco doesn't help. She's
more resigned than knowing. You know?
Can strit-strut whichever whichaway but 'no likee'.

The sages can plod up their ivory mountain
– a few tricky bits where a piton wouldn't go amiss –
to another day on the heights.
But another day on the heights.

Late night who cares. You know?
The buildings obscure in the darkness and
the music folds out. I kiss your sweating cheek.
No servants to summon. No bells to ring.

I like your black boots, but this isn't a love song.
Your shirt soaked in sweat as you 'lay it down',
tell 'them' 'how it is', or poke their assumption.
Poke what matters, dear man, if then.

But all these blocks of stuff get moved around
and we swagger out into the night
fired with the thoughts and the heat of it all.
And the anger and mirrors feed each other somehow,
feel clear for a moment.

O, O, O, . . . Northern California

O, rarely fingered jade sat on your blue velvet cushion
in the museum showcase.
O, handsome writing book half-bound in crimson leather
with beautifully marbled edges
sat on your exquisite and highly polished desk.
O, world of unused beauties.

Kick a stone, walk along the beach, kick the sea.
The dapper panama hat gathers dust on the cupboard's top
    shelf.
Dreams and more dreams. Brightly flowered vines
and the heady scent of eucalyptus trees that
with time is taken for granted and passes unnoticed.

To decorate one's life with sprays of leaves and vases of
    flowers.
I prepare the vase for you on the marble top of a chest of
    drawers.
It's just right. Will it please you? Will you notice it?
You did. Returning from your long journey
you enter the house, striding in with deeds done
and love.

That picture fades as the outside world crowds in
now. And your business continues.
My business continues.
The bright clear sunlight illuminates the headland.
A dusty pickup-truck stops outside the village store
and the dogs leap out as the driver enters.
People at the bar across the street watch this
with their usual bemused curiosity.

Someone in crisp clothing drives past on their way
out of town with their radio playing.
Through the open car window
fine phrases from an opera float out:
'What new delights!
What sweet sufferings!'

The dream fades. A rustling of the dry grasses
that edge the lagoon. We lost it.
And the business continues,
the daily life downtown 'business as usual'.

Gyorgy Kurtag meets Sandy Berrigan

a song cycle

1

A listless evening sprawls out.
We hardly touch.
Through the half-pulled blinds
lights appear in the apartments opposite.

Slumped in our room
we leaf through books and music.
Neither here nor there.
A heavy heat in the apartment but ice in the streets.

You turn and look at me

2

That thin divide
between courage and stupidity.
To have acted and gained
heaven or a relentless hell;
or to have withdrawn and be
haunted by futile regrets.

The dizzying thoughts that
cut into a daily routine.
'What am I doing here, when . . . ?'
But we grasp the 'known',
the silent days, sat by the kitchen window
staring out across the rooftops at the sea.

Alone in my rooms I have my place,
solitary and silent,   and in the mirror
a face that's mine, self-absorbed
and lost in its mirrors.

3

In a remote village the snow
lies heavy around your cabin,
weighs down the trees' branches.

You dream of spring,
of the orchards in blossom,
of the scent of crushed grass.
You dream of

and the cabin door
groans with the wind

4

Despite it all spring comes
and summer follows.   Now
in amongst dark full trees
your cabin stands dry and open.
The white curtains sway in the breeze.

You lie there alone on your bed
listening to the birdsong outside
and the wind rustling the leaves,
a photograph and a star map beside you.

Some miles away the ochre cliffs and dark blue sea.

5

From capitals to small towns to villages
to remote stretches of countryside or coast.
We fly back and forth like trapped birds.

On the hill tops edging the sea
flocks of birds swirl up in clouds
then descend again into the fields and long grass
then up again and at some unknown signal
suddenly fly south across the sea on their way.
The autumn to be filled with such disappearances,
so much to be packed away.

6

In a winter dream 'I fly to you'.
The wells in the villages are frozen.
The pipes in the apartments are frozen.
Naked heart to heart could warm us,
yet my fears, our fears, freeze us.

7

The full moon heavy and oppressive
over the village. The dusty dreamland
above peopled with letters and imaginings.

I talk to you crowded by my own lies
and our mutual foolishness that gives
glimpses of the heavens.
But in love with being in love,
with feeling precious.

8

At dusk
you stand by the well dreaming.
At dusk
an owl slowly flaps into the yew trees.

You return and quietly work in your room.
You lean into the lamplight to thread a needle.

Above the dark outline of the hills
the full moon rises, mottled, orange,
heavy as our dreams where we talk.
A glimmer of its light runs across the sea
and meadows.

Summer solstice

Farm boys tramp home aching from the fields.
They know where they're going, though don't
as they plod past the decaying mansion
overhung with dark trees and surrounded by damp
  undergrowth.
Two more miles to go and then the familiar lit rooms,
the drawers of known possessions, the familiar smells.
They will wash, eat, and go about their evening business.
But it's all far from being that simple and innocent.
Small heaps of possessions litter the landscape.
Funerals are strategically placed throughout the years.
Even rushes of vague but powerful emotions, dumb love
And feelings that cut mazes in the heart.
They pass the darkening hedges and copses
too tired from their labours to care or notice whatever,
though the next morning it could be changed possibly.
In the spacious rooms of the mansion the wind sighs
under the doors along the staircases
from the stone flagged kitchen to the cramped attics.
'Long ago and far away' a story could begin
but leaves the listeners somehow dissatisfied,
nervous on the edge of their chairs leaning forward
in contorted positions.
                              Waking up one day
they could set off in another direction, fresh and foreign.
They could but seldom do, so cluttered are they
and rightly distrustful of such snap solutions.
                              The farm boys proceed
to the fields, again, or turn to the factory towns.
There are glimpses caught in the dusky woods.

or on a fresh summer dawn of unknown skies,
unforgettable and dazzling in their beauty. But then
the long day stretches ahead. The stirred dreams settle down
with the dust, beyond grasp or understanding.
The unseen night birds calling calling

Index of titles and first lines